The SPIRIT

CARLOS BERNARDO GONZÁLEZ PECOTCHE

(Raumsol)

Editora
LOGOSÓFICA

LATEST PUBLICATIONS BY AUTHOR

An Introduction to Logosophical Cognition, 494 p., 1951. [1] [2] [3]

Logosophical Exegesis, 110 p., 1956. [1] [2] [3] [4]

The Mechanism of Conscious Life, 125 p., 1956. [1] [2] [3] [4] [5]

Self-Inheritance, 32 p., 1957. [1] [2] [3] [4]

Logosophy, Science and Method, 150 p., 1957. [1] [2] [3] [4]

Deficiencies and Propensities of the Human Being, 213 p., 1962. [1] [2] [3] [4]

Initiation Course into Logosophy, 102 p., 1963. [1] [2] [3] [4] [5]

Bases for Your Conduct, 55 p., 1965. [1] [2] [3] [4] [5]

The Spirit, 196 p., 1968. [1] [2] [3] [4] [6]

(1) in Spanish

(2) in Portuguese

(3) in English

(4) in French

(5) in Italian

(6) in Hebrew

The SPIRIT

CARLOS BERNARDO GONZÁLEZ PECOTCHE

(Raumsol)

EDITORA LOGOSÓFICA
2009

Original title
El Espíritu
Carlos Bernardo González Pecotche

Translation
Members of the Logosophical Foundation

Graphic design and production
Adesign

Dados Internacionais de Catalogação na Publicação (CIP)
(Câmara Brasileira do Livro, SP, Brasil)

González Pecotche, Carlos Bernardo, 1901-1963.
    The spirit / Carlos Bernardo González Pecotche
(Raumsol) ; [translated from Spanish by members
of the Logosophical Foundation]. – São Paulo :
Logosófica, 2009.

    Título original: El espíritu
    ISBN 978-85-7097-071-8

    1. Espírito 2. Logosofia I. Título

                                        CDD – 128.2
09-08306   – 149.9

Índices para catálogo sistemático:

1. Espírito : Filosofia 128.2
2. Logosofia : Doutrinas filosóficas 149.9

Copyright **da Editora Logosófica**

www.editoralogosofica.com.br
www.logosofia.org.br
Fone/fax: (11) 3804 1640
Rua General Chagas Santos, 590-A – Saúde
CEP 04146-051– São Paulo-SP – Brasil,
da Fundação Logosófica
Em Prol da Superação Humana

Sede central:
Rua Piauí, 762 – Bairro Santa Efigênia
CEP 30150-320 – Belo Horizonte-MG

When investigation is detained in the frontiers of the transcendent world, it is because common knowledge is insufficient to penetrate it. Science must elevate its eyes above its customary rigidity in order to join the great conceptions of Universal Knowledge.

FOREWORD

Those who read this book will undoubtedly realize that its contents form part of a plan conceived by logosophical wisdom to allow the triumphant penetration of the human being into the mysteries of his existence and to discover the indisputable and unobjectionable truth about everything he is interested in knowing about himself and the metaphysical world.

It is well known that freedom of thought has no worse enemy than one's own limitations, and these are, in particular, the prejudices and the fears generated by inculcated ideas that hinder free reasoning and drown every expression of feeling, which is always anxious to achieve a greater expression via the noble claims of the heart.

Fortunately, many people are willing to exercise their inalienable right to become owners and masters of their own will, of their own intelligence and of their sensitivity; in short, to be in command of their lives and maintain their own destiny subject only to their unique and exclusive dependency.

THE SPIRIT, like all other logosophical books, must be read in a state of mind that seeks, through meditative reading, cognitions that broaden and enrich life. This is to be accomplished with the clear notion of the importance of such an endeavor.

Finally we must point out that the basic words utilized in this book carry logosophical content that differs from the ones used commonly. Therefore, we seek to apply within our own frame of reference the meaning we give to them; for example, when we mention the word "conscious" it will be understood that we refer to the state of plenitude which instills life with a new and vibrant radiance.

One commonly thinks and acts by virtue of a rapid mental process which takes place in the periphery of conscience. Undoubtedly nobody could say that he is conscious during every instant of his life, and especially when concerning that which pertains to his evolution and destiny.

Logosophy has stated that conscience is the live essence of the cognitions that integrate it, which implies *that the greater the number of cognitions it assimilates, greater is the conscious altitude of the individual. However, this will never be sufficient to activate its full function which is achieved when it nourishes itself on cognitions that protect the process of conscious evolution, and when that process, realized under the control of self-observation, warns us of the difference that exists between the common content of the word "conscious" and the logosophical one.*

Man must be conscious of the favorable changes he experiences day after day in his moral, psychological and spiritual states, as well as his growing conscious ability to understand that he can broaden his life indefinitely.

INTRODUCTION

Since the beginning of time man's life has been a continuous journey between ignorance and knowledge, regulated by the progressive development of the functions of his understanding which led him to exert unusual efforts to free himself from the first and reach the second, most of which materialized in the technical and scientific fields as well as in the arts. Nevertheless, there were zones of his mind that remained outside the scope of this evolutionary development. We are referring to the zones that include: 1) self-knowledge, 2) the knowledge of the metaphysical or transcendental world, 3) the knowledge of God.

These mental zones, converted by their inactivity into obstacles that limit one's understanding, became more and more insurmountable due to one's pretension to overcome them by directing one's attention invariably toward the external. That was how man has repeatedly tried to see, study and discover in his fellow men the causes that would reveal his origin, the reason of his appearance on earth, his mission, and finally, his extraterrestrial future, that is, the survival of his psychic being. He could not understand – since nobody gave him this great knowledge – that such a wonderful mystery had to be discovered in the depths of his own inner self, for it is there, and nowhere else that man will reach the long-awaited instant to meet with his spirit and receive from it the immense goodness represented by the awakening to a reality that surpasses all intuition.

It is difficult for the person who has remained uninterested in the knowledge of his spiritual nature to comprehend that in this knowledge lies the explanation of multiple, incomprehensible facts related to his own life and that of his fellow men. Only now, by becoming aware of this reality as Logosophy reveals it to human understanding, can man appear before himself with full knowledge and assert himself as the conscious master of his existence. He will then realize with astonishment why certain important sectors of mankind fall victim to error as they are led through the tortuous paths of fantasy, invented to shackle them to obscure beliefs.

Man cannot alienate the freedom of his spirit unless he does so at the risk of thwarting his evolution and losing his individuality. He must therefore preserve this freedom from all risks; and he will be successful if he unites with his spirit by means of the process of conscious evolution as prescribed and taught by the logosophical science.

Our conception of the spirit begins by explaining what its essence and its precise and unobjectionable reality are, how it influences the being it animates, what is its prerogative, its possibility of manifestation and finally, its true mission here, in this vast experimental field which is the world. Its explanation, however, requires a true didactic effort which must not omit any concrete detail especially if it is meant to guide one's understanding toward acquiring an ample and tenacious practice with the aim of comprehending unequivocally the huge significance of a cognition of such magnitude as the one contained in the integral conception of the spirit.

This, of course, takes time. We point this out because of the general tendency of wanting to know it all at once whether by simply reading through or by glancing over the stated truth founded on categorical facts. The knowledge of one's spirit demands above all seriousness, serene meditations, continuous and thorough analysis of its fleeting interventions and constant attention to the need to surprise it when it uses our faculties. Concrete examples of its brief interventions are present every time we see emerging in our mind valuable thoughts whose contribution was unexpected, or when brilliant ideas that amaze our own judgment surge as a result of the act of thinking.

In this kind of studies, therefore, there is no place for haste or neglect which are invariably detrimental to the success of the investigations that will culminate in unfailing and concrete proof regarding the authentic reality of the spirit as the intelligent and dynamic power of human existence.

We know that it is generally difficult to supplant an almost unmodifiable concept deeply rooted in the mind by another. To some, for instance, the spirit is the soul or the intellect or the psychic center of thought. To others, it is the incorporeal being, the act of reasoning, the sensitivity and even the personality. There are some who even believe that the spirit manifests itself in the emotional, sentimental or soaring intellectual and artistic state as proof that by momentarily exalting his lofty pleasures man concedes to his spirit the prerogative to be entertained with such preferences. This is a regrettable error as will be seen later when we thoroughly describe some circumstances regarding the modalities that characterize the spirit. We must, however, state at this time that notwithstanding the difficulty pointed out, we were able to appreciate how quickly this was removed by those who, using their own reasoning and not the reasoning of others, have acknowledged the substantial differences that exist between the confused common concept and the clear and precise logosophical conception.

If we insist on this matter it is because we know the distance that exists between the mind and the true concept contained in the word "spirit". Nobody has stated it explicitly, because none have penetrated the secrets of its undemonstrative yet nonetheless wonderful reality. We have said "undemonstrative", because it is an unquestionable truth that man does not have the evidence of its reality since he has not experienced the changes that are produced in him when the spirit is disposed to integrate man's psychophysical structure and actively participate in managing his life. Truly, the spirit has been ignored or referred to with prejudice, and in many cases it has been systematically negated – we are referring here to science – as if the spirit were something impossible to prove or foreign to the investigation of this branch of human knowledge. We do not even refer to the millions of souls who have not gone beyond the most elementary levels of culture and who have not the remotest idea of what the spirit is and what it must represent to each individual.

Inasmuch as we are giving important elements of judgment to allow everyone to form a precise concept of his spirit, as he must know it and feel it in its manifest reality, we must warn that this will never happen by merely reading what we express, but rather by the rational and conscious application of such cognitions to the internal process that Logosophy teaches to establish; a process by which real and concrete changes can be verified as the definitive proof of this truth. Therefore, we wish to emphasize that it would be naïve and self-deceiving to anyone who would pretend to satisfy his inquietude by the mere theoretical knowledge of a subject that must represent transcendental importance to life.

C.B.G.P.

PART ONE

The Spirit

Three Preliminary Questions

As a real and active being, man's spirit no longer seems to bepart of our concerns.

Why have so many millennia passed without a statement regarding its real specific function?

What hidden designs conceal its great secret?

Why should man remain indifferent to the reality of his own spirit?

By presenting its thesis on this transcendental issue, Logosophy reveals the profound moral meaning contained in the knowledge of the life of the spirit.

Chapter 1

ORIGIN OF SPIRITUAL INQUIETUDES

It is natural for man to worry about the beyond about his extra physical destiny, an inquietude that intensifies every now and then as a result of suffering when faced with enigmas that his intelligence has sought in vain to explain. The specter of death terrifies him. He looks at his physical being and trembles at the thought that he may lose it, that he will lose it irrevocably and he has asked himself with repeated anxiety if it were possible to escape from this imagined vortex that inexorably leads him to the total disintegration of his existence. His intelligence does not answer, it remains silent, but internally the inquietude deepens and sometimes reaches the point of anxiety.

What else but one's own spirit promotes such anxiety? What else, if not the spirit, induces man to seek knowledge? Not the common knowledge that satisfies the demands of the common life. We are referring to the knowledge that enriches the conscience, which transcends the ordinary sphere of the world, a knowledge intended to govern, according to its development, the immense mental field, the metaphysical, populated by the thoughts and the great ideas. It is in this environment of countless millions of extra physical entities that the individual spirit usually captures the most valuable images which it shares with the physical entity when an intimate correspondence between them, aimed at achieving full identification, is established.

In a way, one could compare the physical entity to a television set with an antenna. Without it the images are blurred, but with it they become clear. In the case of the physical entity no one will have doubts about what represents the antenna except that it is a mobile antenna not a fixed one, and as such is far-reaching when it increases its receptive capability, in other words, when the spirit, escalating the heights of evolution, covers ever widening areas of the universal conception.

It so happens that when man experiences these

inquietudes he seeks to satisfy them without thinking that they require the participation of his reasoning and his sensitivity in order to feel the need to address his integral emancipation[1]. In this way he can only soothe or, better still, temporarily sedate his will which should be stimulated by an energetic yearning for self-improvement. At this point, we must mention the disappointment experienced by countless people who, in all good faith, believed they had found the means to satisfy their inquietudes by going from one place to another and turning to those who had nothing to offer except their extravagant ideas, their beliefs or their ambitions for profit. Even religion, as well as science and philosophy, also has been alien to the cognitions related to the spirit and consequently has not been able to properly guide the believer to help him overcome his difficulties.

Faced with these results, one can state with assurance that very little or nothing at all in fact has been said regarding the human spirit; furthermore, one may go so far as to say that to this day nobody has

---

[1] The integral emancipation includes the mental, moral, psychic and spiritual parts which in turn free the physical part from its impotence.

addressed the issue with the necessary seriousness and certainty. Those who took upon themselves the responsibility to elucidate this question – either on their own volition or by a mandate given to them by their respective philosophical or religious communities – have never been able to satisfy such a noble inquietude precisely because they lacked the cognitions that would reveal to them the profound mystery that the spirit must represent to man's reasoning.

When the individual reaches this conclusion, he rebels against all such meaningless eloquence and becomes morally resentful. Nevertheless, and in spite of everything, he continues searching. His hopes prevail for a long time before they extinguish and yet in the midst of so much darkness and error he always feels confident he will find a light that will illuminate his intelligence.

Had man been created only of "clay", as has been often repeated, he would have had as many inquietudes as the creature that belongs to the other species. But the constant yearning for self-expression, to communicate, demonstrates the opposite. It demonstrates that his being is not entirely material, that something superior animates his life and allows him to think and feel; it is like something that he can neither see nor touch, but that nevertheless he suspects, senses, or has the intuition of its existence.

This ignored entity which articulates its movements in the mental shadow of the human being, thwarting the queries made by his intelligence, is the spirit, which will, notwithstanding, participate in man's life as soon as man prepares himself to enlighten his intelligence with the necessary cognitions that not only allow him to have access to his inner world but will reveal to him the reason for these inquietudes which he was never able to silence.

In spite of his disappointment, man has always sought to transcend the limitations imposed by the world that surrounds him, requiring him to address its needs by shedding his own light, all of which, however, does not prevent the passing of life while this light dims away without having been able to illuminate other horizons, those that his intuition has so often surmised.

Logosophy discloses endless means to guide man's thought toward the causes that bind him to this situation, but in order for him to benefit from such a discovery, he must be: willing to modify a habit, ingrained in him, of behaving in accordance with his immediate conveniences not knowing with certainty what he is seeking or why he is seeking it. The fact is that most people question themselves about this without overcoming the vagueness of their own questions.

We now take great satisfaction in announcing the transcendent significance of the logosophical contribution which has been confirmed by endless live testimonies. In fact, logosophic truth is of such essential interest to the intelligence and sensitivity of those who receive our teaching – be they children, youngsters or adults – that they instantly assimilate it with joy, for it is felt as a vital nourishment of the existence.

According to statements made by those who experienced it, they refer to it as something about which they had a vague intuition but without ever having found the leverage point or the guiding light that could fully satisfy this inquietude. The importance of the above-mentioned fact should be noted because it is a faithful exponent of the general state of mind of the majority of human beings.

What have religion, philosophy and science said in this regard? Judging by the multiple versions available regarding the spirit, nothing of a concrete nature has established the fundamentals of a reality that can be proven by each individual, free from any suggestion, pressure or influence which in many cases dominate the individual's will.

Nothing would please God more than the pure, sincere and honest yearning for knowing the truth. However, in order to know the truth in each of the parts that subdivide into innumerable steps that ascend to it, one must gradually eliminate everything that simulates truth and is accepted as such. It is fair, therefore, to choose to be, above all, loyal to one's own con-science seeking its contact so that the intelligence can reflect and judge with accuracy every fact, every situation, every word or circumstance related to one's own existence.

Undeniably, all human beings love life; they want to live it even though the majority does not know what to do to live it well. And thus, the days, the months and the years go by as if empty. What does the time of their existence, therefore, amount to? It is different when one lives with intensity, when mind maintains permanent contact with the Universal Thought and feels that one's existence is animated by this thought; life, therefore, takes on another character; it does not feel lonely nor empty. This inner emptiness, which so many people feel without knowing how to fill it, has disappeared.

Previously we made reference to the human being's eagerness to silence the insistent demands of his spirit, expressed by his need to inquire, which we observe in him from birth till the moment he abandons the world. As a result of our own experience, coupled with the observations made by others, we know that even a child, when given an answer that satisfies his anxieties, experiences a pleasant sensation of calm; he has filled the emptiness created by his inquietude. What is wrong and harmful, we repeat, is when the child, reaching adulthood, is unable to properly address his anxieties and accumulates within himself all of what he ignores, but whose existence is perceived by his senses or his intuition, and is expressed in the intimate need to be happier than he is, and in the anxiety of grasping a broader notion of life. How many false steps would be avoided if one were only to understand that the manifestation of such inquietudes have their origin in the same force that sustains human life, and in recognizing that it is one's own spirit which is responsible for keeping them alive until man decides to address seriously this inner call, which even though is not pressing in every ease, nevertheless hovers over life.

As the knowledgeable expert of the causes which continuously stimulate man in his march through life, Logosophy offers him the opportunity to accomplish in himself this great alchemical transformation, which by means of a process of conscious evolution allows him to develop aptitudes that control and regulate his aspirations, all of which creates a state of equilibrium propitious for the manifestations of the spirit. Hence, our insistence in demanding that the necessary attention be paid to these cognitions which, being of a transcendental nature, consciously guide thoughts and actions, and offer the spirit the opportunity of living on earth with similar prerogatives to those of his physical being.

Chapter 2

TRANSCENDENT COGNITION

The fundamental principle of transcendent knowledge states that the great cosmic experience cognition descends from the supreme to the human and ascends from the human to the supreme. The vast space between both positions is filled by Creation, where the universal life palpitates, where all the processes of nature develop, and where God's Thought lives permanently.

Everything that is engraved in this wonderful Universal Science, contained in the Great Cosmic Mind, had one Supreme objective: that of getting to be known by all the off-springs created with sufficient intelligence to comprehend the infinite diversity of its parts by means of the process of conscious evolution that all would have to achieve.

In other words, God's Wisdom is engraved in the Creation, while man's wisdom consists in getting to know it and use it to escalate the evolutionary steps of his kind.

The transcendent cognition therefore, descends, from incommensurable cosmic heights down to man, who must gradually get to know God's Thought in each one of the manifestations offered to his intelligence by Creation. In his progress towards this objective he will first cross the valleys that lay before him, he will then ascend the parts that are more or less rugged and rough, until he climbs one by one, ever more surely and with greater balance, the great summits of knowledge.

While transcendent cognitions regulate the forces that sustain the action of thoughts and feelings exalting the souls, and highlight both the traits of the heart and the expressions of an illuminated intelligence, the other cognitions, the common ones, those that are not transcendental, adjust to the limitations of the human mind as a necessity to address the daily sustenance and to contribute to the discoveries that improve this same sustenance.

In most cases, man thinks and feels in a limited manner, resigned to a life made indifferent as a result of his habits and customs; but he can, if he so determines, overcome these limitations and penetrate vast unsuspected zones as he identifies' himself with the universal life of which he is a part.

Why does man seek knowledge if it were not his intuition that indicates it to be the means to find happiness? Undoubtedly it is because his presentiment detects the attractive perspectives offered to him when, determined to jump over the fence which limits his life's horizon, he succeeds in transporting himself to other levels where thoughts take on new forms, offer greater values to his understanding, enabling him to elevate himself and inviting him to permanently advance. It is there, in those regions where the spirit travels fully conscious, that man feels the power of cognition, and the sensation of greatness that permeates him is such, that life itself seems transformed and becomes unexpectedly transparent.

Since physical life is a small period of man's existence through the ages, it is logical for him to aspire to live successfully during these periods and demonstrate what he is able to conquer in them when his thought unites, even partially, with the eternal principles emanating from the dawn of Creation. He then perceives emerging from the innermost depth of his being the force that will immortalize him, since he would be experiencing eternity within himself as Universal Life palpitates; in other words, he elevates his life and converts it into a power capable of illuminating the lives of others who live only, as he once did, in the present, uninterested in the future, and indifferent to the significance of their human condition.

We have no doubt that man seeks knowledge because his own nature demands it, needs it, and moves him towards it, in order to reach higher pinnacles from which he will be able to clearly contemplate the infinite colorings of Creation; he seeks knowledge because it is the great creative agent that allows him to broaden the prerogatives of his existence; he seeks it because it is a new life grafted to his, a life that the spirit breathes in and finds in knowledge the path of its freedom. Finally, man seeks knowledge because it is the means by which he is able to understand his mission and feel the presence in his life of this immaterial being which responds to the influence of the eternal Universal Conscience and which is the bearer of individual existence throughout time.

Chapter 3

ENIGMA — GENESIS OF THE ASCENDANCY OF THE SPECIES: THE 4TH REALM

Even though man's intuition senses that his origin comes from God's Creative Thought, author of his archetypal perfection, the spiritual one, by an illogical anachronism has insisted for a long time that he consider himself a derivative of an inferior being: the "missing link", which surely determines his obscure ascendancy. Unaware that this would not satisfy the intimate aspirations of his spirit, man plunged into a long, passionate, but sterile adventure, since the real link, the one that should particularly interest him is that which links man to his Creator. This is the missing link.

The difference that exists between man and the animal kingdom is as pronounced as the difference that appears "in extenso" between the mineral and the vegetable kingdoms, and between the latter and the animal realm. It is determined by the fact that even the most advanced representatives of the animal realm do not have a spirit. Instinct in animals takes on intelligent and sensitive forms that appear according to the traits that characterize each species. The animal lacks true sensitivity because suffering or moral pain does not exist in it. Its pain is instinctive as when its litter is withdrawn, or when it demonstrates its attachment to its missing masters. Consequently, what most enhances man's difference and superiority in relation to the animal is, as we have already mentioned, his spirit and all its inherent prerogatives.

The prehistoric existence of the *australopithecus* or the *pithecanthropus* and lately the *telanthropus* have been considered in vain as possible predecessors or missing links of the human family[1]. This is a regrettable error made by scientists who, instead of conducting their investigation towards their inner

[1] See "Mister De Sandara" by the same author (page 474).

selves to discover in their spirits the enigma, genesis of the ascendance of our species, remain obstinate in seeking a connection with inferior species, an unnecessary link to understand, or to sense at least, the true origin of man.

Logosophical science discards this theory as sterile, and, undeterred by man's feverish search to snatch away the mystery of his origin held secretly in custody by his past, opens up a new avenue of investigation, inviting man to penetrate it and, in subsequent conquests, deliver him one day into God's hands.

Possibly, Phylogeny based its theory on this error, or has inadvertently made it, when its representatives included human kind in the animal realm; that is to say that the scientist, who is ultimately a man, included himself as an integral part of the zoological ladder.

Logosophy bestows hierarchy upon man by proclaiming the fourth realm, which differs vastly from the others. Its psychic constitution includes its praiseworthy mental[2], sensitive[3],

---

[2] The **Mental System** is made up of two minds: the superior and the inferior, and both are constituted equally, but differ in function and prerogatives. The first is reserved for the spirit which makes use of it when one's conscience awakens to the

and instinctive[4] systems, and if this were not enough, the excellencies of his spirit, all of which are lacking in all other living creatures of the interior realms, and position man, with undeniable justice, in a superior realm by itself that we have named "human".

reality that connects it to the transcendent or metaphysical world. The objective of the second is to take care of the material needs of the physical entity or soul, and one's conscience may intervene in its activities. Both minds, the superior and the inferior, have exactly the same mechanism, constituted by the faculties of thinking, of reasoning, of judging, intuition, of understanding, of observing, of imagining, of remembering, of predicting, etc., which are assisted in their activities by other faculties, which we will call accessories, whose functions are to discern, reflect. combine, etc. All the faculties form the intelligence. Logosophy denominates the latter as the summit faculty because it encompasses all of them. (Logosophy: Science and Method. Lesson III)

[3] The **Sensitive System** is a constituent part of the human soul and has its seat in the heart, an eminently sensitive organ and the regulating center of man's psychical life. It is divided into two fields or zones, each clearly defined. One pertains to the Sensitivity, consisting of the faculties of feeling, of wanting, of loving, of suffering, of compassion, of gratitude, of consenting, and of forgiving. The other zone belongs to the feelings: it is the dimensional space in which these are born, live, and operate. (Logosophy: Science and Method. Lesson V.)

[4] Constituted as a system, the instinct makes up one of three parts into which the psychological energies of the individual are divided; the two others correspond to the mental and sensitive systems. Besides its specific generative function, the instinct is characterized by the ardent manifestations that its activity always unleashes upon human nature. The energies of the instinct are utilized with great results in the individual's self-improvement when they come into contact with the mental and sensitive energies, consciously activated, since they contribute to the strengthening of the forces of the spirit and cooperate in achieving the successive tasks imposed by the process of conscious evolution. (Logosophy: Science and Method. Lesson VI.)

Chapter 4

THE LOGOSOPHICAL CONCEPTION OF GOD

According to logosophic thought, God is the immensity, the eternal; He is the Supreme Science of Wisdom that the human mind can discover in each of the universal processes that are embedded in nature, such processes are precise, pure and perfect science, which inspire man to create "his" science.

God's Thought is manifested in Creation in whose womb beats the love He placed in it and whose power sustains it. His love is one that towers far above all other loves and is revealed in everything that exists; a love that animates life in the universality of its manifestations, a love that never dies, never deceives; a love that surges from the very depth of nature to encourage us, to impel us, and touches us deeply when faced with the immanence of everything that is given to us to contemplate in the universe. With this same love, He also made the human being and bestowed upon him the privilege of presenting to Him, one day, as an offering, the great accomplishments that will make of his life, this very life that He has given him to live and enjoy, something useful for himself and for his fellow men.

Logosophy situates God in the highest seat, a place to which the foolishness of men, who are determined to confine him to the narrowness of their mental conceptions, will never ascend. Logosophy proclaims the existence of a Universal God who unites all men in the one and only religion; the religion of knowledge, which is the means to ascend to Him, to understand Him, to feel Him, and love Him; never through ignorance.

It is well known that man has always searched for his metaphysical bond with God; hence the origin of the religions, of the philosophies, and of all the ancient and modern rites and cults. Man always had an intuition that beyond the physical there exists equally an impenetrable greatness, which moved him to travel an infinite number of paths always searching for the key that would bring him closer to

Him. Regrettably, he had to conform himself with faith which, when it is not the fruit of profound conviction, enlightened by knowledge, foments fanaticism that makes it impossible for the human spirit to link with the Great Universal Spirit.

It is inconceivable to the logosophical conception that the human being could confine God to a statue, a house, a country, a continent, a planet, or even the entire universe, since it considers all of this to be too limited and narrow to contain the dimensions of His August Image, which is too great for the human mind. It is generally recognized, however, and more than justified, that everybody, even the most hardened atheist, seeks to know of Him. What is it, if not the human mind that continually inquires, going from one point to another, although unconsciously, about the motions of its anguish? Do we not seek God in moments of affliction and every time we face great difficulties in our own march through life? Is He not sought in religions? Do we not investigate and carefully study ancient books with this objective, does not man penetrate the labyrinths of the pyramids and does he not attempt to discover life in other worlds in outer space? Is he not tormented when, after believing that he found Him, his conscience refuses to bestow upon the finding the certainty required?

Throughout history, we have come to learn about the evolution of the species, the wonderful movements of the stars, the different periods that disciplined the progress of mankind through the ages, following the processes of development that obey the dictates of the Supreme Intelligence whose power reaches out to the fringes of Creation. If we consider that God differentiated man from the other terrestrial creatures and endowed him with unlimited possibilities of psychological and spiritual elevation, then we must consider that from this unconscious process that he undertakes without individual verification of the successes or errors produced in his behavior as they relate to the lofty aims of his existence, that he could by self-determination alone, create consciously the bond with his Creator, which can be achieved through self-knowledge, which allows him to gradually grasp the divine architecture of his inner world, and at the same time grants him the graciousness of getting to know God. This is why we will not cease to reiterate that the most extraordinary knowledge, the greatest that man can possess, is primarily and fundamentally the knowledge of this human creature, who is his own self. The study of man highlights the most wonderful creation: man himself molded in the image of Creation.

One may ask what would have been God's objective in placing in the world a race of beings so intelligently endowed, who would ignore him and live on the fringes of Universal Creation. Could one, for an instant, think that He would accomplish such a stupendous act of His Will so that man, to whom he gave psychological and spiritual faculties of extraordinary reach, would be satisfied with little more than wandering through the world extraneous to the lofty aims of his existence? Certainly not. It is necessary to understand therefore that man must learn to know God in order to truly love Him; to know His laws so as not to infringe them; to shape his conduct in line with the supreme dictates of His Will so that His Great Spirit can assist him during the long evolutionary process that man must undergo throughout time.

God has His altar in the bosom of Creation, and He has it also in every human heart. In the former, officiate the cosmic powers; in the latter, the individual conscience. It is in this altar, that the soul formulates its queries, clarifies its doubts, perceives the presence of the spirit, and each time determines higher levels of behavior. In this altar the soul bows in sweet rapture, full of gratitude, until it reaches ecstasy, the expression of the most intimate and happy emotions, because what is ecstasy if not the exaltation of happiness in moments of supreme psychic balance, when thought and feeling blend into one flame, alive and potent, while the conscience regulates the power of inner expansion?

God's Spirit is the Supreme Cosmic Expression, because the universal energy vibrates within it. It is revealed to man in the immanence of its own nature, in the inviolability of its laws and in its intelligence, which animates and sustains the perpetuity of Creation.

Chapter 5

THE METAPHYSICAL WORLD

Much has been said about heaven. It has been described as having marvelous colors and as being destined for the blessed; but of what use can a place be if nobody knows nor has ever known it, and of which no one has any real reference?

In response to this inquisitive attitude of the human being that moves him to investigate beyond what is perceptible to his corporeal senses, Logosophy places within his reach not only a heaven that is different, but also prepares him to penetrate it without ever getting lost. This heaven is the metaphysical world.

We refer implicitly to the process of conscious evolution which, as it introduces man to the domain of his own inner world, allows him, from the start, become acquainted with the influence of the metaphysical or transcendent world, which is the natural environment of the lofty ideas, thoughts and the energy that palpitates in the existence of all Creation. In so doing, it enlightens him appropriately and offers him an aggregate of recommendations that orient him through an extremely interesting journey which begins in the depths of his being and extends broadly towards infinity.

The entry into the inner individual world allows the connection with the metaphysical world to occur. Both form an inseparable unit to which man must adapt by positioning himself within it and seeking resources to consolidate it in the unique part where they can be formed: in self-knowledge, through which he becomes conscious of what he is, what he possesses, of what he can and must be, and by getting to know the goodness of the metaphysical world and its beauty, which he will admire with growing amazement. Self-knowledge, therefore, is the knowledge that the soul aspires to obtain from its own spirit; the path that is conducive to the encounter and the link with the metaphysical world, which does not in any way constitute a

Utopia, but rather a reality that is proportionately verifiable to the fertile effort made by man towards improving his behavior in all areas of his life.

Access to the metaphysical world, unexplored by man in spite of his attempts and the multiple hypotheses ventured on the subject, determines the gradual transfer of the spirit's inheritance into the individual's hands. In other words, this implies the identification of the physical entity or soul with the spirit, and logically constitutes a considerable progress in the process of conscious evolution.

We repeat that the knowledge of the metaphysical world starts, indispensably, with self-knowledge, since both worlds, the inner self and the metaphysical, are indissolubly bound. We should, at this point, highlight the valuable function of the spirit as the guide that leads us into the world of great ideas, where God's Thought reigns permanently. This is why Logosophy indicates the spirit as being the link that unites man to his Creator. It should be noted that we are delving into the secrets of an enigma which to this day has remained impenetrable to human understanding, and that we do so with the same clarity as we have always used in expressing our thoughts.

We also think we have clearly established that the knowledge of one's inner world leads to the knowledge of the metaphysical world and, in so doing, offers the prerogative of knowing one's own spirit, the one that will introduce us into it.

The metaphysical world must be regarded with the same reality as the physical one, and one must march to meet it not only for the assets it provides, but mainly because of the energies that the person who aspires knowledge generates through his own efforts while evolving. In doing so, one must be aware that next to the metaphysical world, and etched by the same supreme laws, there exists a subjacent zone in which all those who pretend to know the metaphysical world without having first detained their capricious flights of fantasies, run the risk of going astray. This is the zone of illusion, the chimerical zone which provides foolhardy confusion about the metaphysical world; the hurdle that emerges in the path of those who have not sought protection from the laws of knowledge before delving into it.

We have seen throughout history that it was always knowledge that allowed man to surpass the levels achieved by each prior civilization, leaving as a tribute to human progress the revelation of many mysteries. It behooves the men of today to go even beyond that, not only by penetrating the inexplorable chasms of the cosmos, but also by investigating the depths of the mental world and extracting from it the live elements that enrich the spirit. In exploring these depths man will discover the mysteries related to his origin, and they will be revealed to him in all their splendor, the yet undecipherable enigmas of the human mind and we will see rekindled the almost faded hopes for a better destiny.

In undertaking this endeavor it should be noted that the mental or metaphysical world is not accessible to the soul. The nature of the latter is not subtle and incorporeal as is the nature of the spirit, which is equipped to pass through the doors of this world, which are also incorporeal. The soul could participate in the benefits it receives, it could be the receptacle of all the notions transmitted by the spirit, but the soul itself, on its own account, will never have access. Prior to that it must propitiate in the individual the intervention of the spirit, which by virtue of the law of correspondence, will allow it, in an everwidening scope, to participate in the lofty conceptions of the transcendent world that is its world, the world of the spirit.

Man often places the divine in sublime levels whilst he remains in the darkness of a voluntary moral and spiritual seclusion. This would be admissible if he did not have a spirit and if, in his mind, were not reflected every now and then, unequivocal signs of a superiority that borders the regions where he supposes the divine can only exist. Nevertheless, to concede that the divine is beyond human possibilities, to concede that it is inaccessible, would be to negate capability and hierarchy to the great souls.

God's Wisdom has determined that the truths which connect man to his spirit remain locked up inside his being. And there they lie in waiting, until they are discovered, for which man must penetrate within his own self, and from there get to know the metaphysical world: the cause and origin of all that exists.

MAN AND HIS TWO NATURES

When God created earthly man, his conception was perfect, as it could not be otherwise. He made him superior to any other living being on earth, and in so doing, he granted him the grace to possess two natures, physical and spiritual. This clearly explains the survival of the human spirit, since as the physical life ceases to exist, the spiritual life remains formed by the eternal elements that constitute the existence.

The physical nature, endowed with a perfect organism that has an automatic and permanent function that acts independently of the will, having devices and biological systems that act and intercommunicate between themselves in a marvelous way, and a psychological mechanism that is summarized in the soul, has fulfilled and will continue to fulfill its human mission within the needs, limitations and perspectives that belong to the life of man, whom someone called, somewhat prematurely, "king of creation". And we say "someone", because nobody can ascertain the veracity of this version that grants such a high ranking without the required merits. Within this physical nature, which constitutes the material base of human existence, a considerable part of his highest conception was molded, allowing his kind to be superior creatures, but that part, with its admirable biological organization, only aims to articulate life based on material needs and perspectives.

It will be understood from the aforementioned that the physical nature is perishable and it is so due to its corruptibility which culminates in its disintegration, a fact that we should point out, does not occur with the spirit, whose nature is immutable. But the evolutionary changes that beget perpetuity are not produced in it, but rather in the hereditary cell, mental substance, basic and eminently sensitive, which continue to shape the individual destiny of each man.

The spiritual nature of man, that is, the one that corresponds to his spirit, differs from the physical in that it is incorporeal and imperishable. The human being must understand that all his efforts must be directed towards the predominance of his spiritual nature in order to experience in his conscience the exact sensation of perenniality.

Thus, he will reach the consubstantiation of both natures, the physical and the spiritual, that is, the harmonious conjunction of two differently constituted organisms: one of a superior and pure mental essence, the other, physical, inferior, subject to the influence of the first, but without this predominance altering, as one would expect, its normal psychobiological manifestations; to the contrary, the spiritual part is a balancing factor between both parts, which have been created to complement each other admirably. One will appreciate the importance of knowing this duality which constitutes the human structure, whose mechanism is capable of joining both parts and gravitating with amazing results over the life of the individual.

How can this mechanism be articulated? Herein lies the great question. Clearly it will not be by virtue of a miracle or by special grace. Man must learn to organize his life in order to perpetuate himself within his own conscience, for it is the conscience that allows man to experience the ineffable sensation of being and of existing, and which concentrates in the hereditary or genetic cell, the perfect synthesis of everything he accomplished during his life. All the conquests achieved in favor of self-improvement are therein imprinted, thus contributing to perpetuate the inheritance and represent the true identity of the individual-such assets becoming his exclusive ownership in which even his own features are imprinted.

The hereditary or genetic cell is, therefore, the carrier of the spiritual inheritance of each individual. In it are deposited the intellectual, moral and spiritual values that man incorporates during each one of the stages of human life throughout his long existence, and similarly, everything that he has done wrong during those periods of life. The individual spirit is the trustee of said inheritance, which man disposes at will in each existential stage and enjoys, according to the direction in which he decides to steer his life, the progress achieved; or, has to bear the errors that have slowed him down and detained him. The hereditary cell, which is always collected and retained by the spirit, advances through the generations, but remains a secret to man until he discovers, as a result of the reencounter with his own spirit, the values of the individual patrimony accumulated throughout his existence.

As the spirit is the unique depository of our long lasting assets and the reason for being of our conscious existence which has been maintained whole in its essential individuality throughout all the cycles of its course, it will not be difficult to understand how necessary it is for the physical being or soul to get accustomed to feel the influx of its spiritual nature exactly as it experiences that of its psychobiological nature, that is to say, as an unavoidable imperative. Soon one will be able to see that one nature is as real as the other, and that by familiarizing himself with the first, man will clarify the incognita of his mysterious biopsychospiritual conformation.

Related to the domains of the spirit and consubstantial to it, are the mental and sensitive systems of the individual, his thoughts and ideas, his perceptions and every expression manifested by the physical being in its psychic form, characterized by the soul.

It would never be too much to call attention to the admirable creation that is man himself. In spite of his frequently slovenly conduct which would seem to negate this, man was created without omitting any of the details that make him a being fit to successfully undertake the great experiment that leads him to penetrate the domains of conscious evolution.

Logosophy places within the reach of his intelligence the transcendental cognitions which are precisely the ones that introduce him into this zone, so rarely frequented and accessible only to the spirit, and permanently stimulate his yearnings for betterment, allowing him to conquer, step by step, levels of consciousness in line with the living reality of his spirit. When man achieves this, he carries within himself not only the memories but also the inner presence of his entire existence, that is to say, having become consubstantial with his spirit, he has also consubstantiated himself with his existence throughout the ages, and at that point, the knowledge of his self-inheritance is no longer forbidden to him.

Chapter 7

DETERMINATION AND OUTLINE
OF THE SOUL

In examining the concept of the soul and the identification attributed to it with regard to the spirit, to the point of confounding them in a strange synonymity, we feel obliged to determine the exact position of the soul with its specific faculties and its connection with the spirit.

The soul is the physical entity in its psychological configuration. It animates, incites to action, and develops the three systems – the mental, the sensitive and the instinctive – but its function is limited to the common human prerogatives, that is, in the material, moral, and intellectual spheres. The soul uses intelligence, sensitivity, and instinct in all emergencies and questions related to the development of physical life, including its highest intellectual aspects. Coherent with its physical being, it intervenes actively in man's biological development. When the breath of life disappears, both body and soul cease to exist. This does not occur with the spirit, since its existence does not depend on what is material.

Due to the nature of its constitution, the soul is inseparable from the physical being. For this reason, when life ceases in the latter, the soul accompanies the body in its disintegration; it is, therefore, perishable. As we shall see later on, its lasting memories left in others in recognition of its merits does not modify the aforementioned.

By destroying with its affirmations the so-called immortality of the soul and proclaiming the immortality of the spirit, Logosophy does no more than place things in their proper perspective. It is therefore not a question of simply changing words, but rather of determining functions, without depriving the soul of its paramount role as an irreplaceable agent within the system, destined to harmoniously coordinate man's physical, psychic, and spiritual activities.

When the spirit acts in full harmony with the soul, life is not only endowed with beauty, but all of it becomes a clear demonstration of the transforming effects brought about by the transcendent cognition, which, confirmed by the conscience, generates a growing activity that always protects the principles of goodness emerging from its essence.

Logosophy establishes totally new and revolutionary concepts regarding the soul and the spirit, indicating a substantial difference between both. As we said, the soul integrates the physical entity in its psychological part; notwithstanding the fact of its autonomous entity and full freedom of movement, the spirit is linked to the soul or physical being as long as the latter exists in its human structure. By virtue of its eternal essence and because it carries the hereditary wealth of the individual it animates, it is destined to develop a transcendent influence over the physical and psychological part of the individual.

The process of conscious evolution established by Logosophy leads man to understand that when he transcends the frontiers which limit his comprehension, when he penetrates beyond the realm of current knowledge, it is his spirit and not his soul that uses his intelligence, his sensitivity, and his energetic resources to develop superior aptitudes. Such a valuable prerogative demands from him to be conscious of it and to know that it is the result of a process of reuniting him with his spirit through the gradual understanding and experimental verification of its metaphysical reality.

Chapter 8

OUTLINE OF THE SPIRIT AS THE NATURAL LINKING AGENT BETWEEN MAN AND THE CREATOR

The vague and contradictory references made with regard to the spirit have led man to consider it as something of an abstraction, something beyond the reach of his reasoning and feeling. Furthermore, he committed the error of accepting as truths certain absurd hypotheses that have nothing to do with the real essence of the spirit and its reality, which can be perfectly proven.

When we stated elsewhere that the spirit remains absent from the being it animates, we wanted to highlight its minute participation in the functions that govern human life, which does not imply its absolute absence, but rather a clear and understandable inhibition.

For Logosophy, the spirit takes on the most important and fundamental role:

a) In the development of human aptitudes.

b) In maintaining a firm and regular functioning of the faculties of the intelligence.

c) In the proliferation of ideas and thoughts of high value.

d) In the enrichment of one's conscience by constantly contributing with cognitions of a transcendent nature.

e) In the fact of surviving when life ceases in the physical being, since it is the spirit that gathers and perpetuates the existence of man without losing his individuality in each cycle of corporeal manifestation.

We must point out that this important and fundamental role of the spirit in man's life can only be accomplished when man provides the necessary conditions for its manifestation and development, since its function is above the physical entity or soul, and the energies it emanates are those that strengthen him to conduct his life according to the lofty objectives of his existence.

We have already stated that, when physical life

ceases, the spirit gathers and carries away imprinted in the mental, hereditary, or genetic cell the historical synthesis that it extracts from the conscience of the physical being it integrated, the value of which depends on the opportunities that it was offered to manifest itself and that will allow it to govern his life in its superior forms of existence. If previous behavior led to lofty accomplishments in every new period of existence, one's spirit delivers the balance of these accomplishments, the accumulated inner reserves, everything the individual was capable of achieving and nothing more. It should therefore be understood that the contribution made by the soul at the end of its days, in knowledge and experience obtained from the common sphere, is absorbed and preserved by one's spirit and will only serve in successive cycles of existence for similar common purposes which the physical life gained and enjoyed. On the other hand, the cognitions and experiences in which one's spirit intervened directly – in addition to the hereditary contribution – grow in volume and become consubstantial with the imperishable existence of the universal thought and mind without losing one's individuality, shielded by its adaptation to its metaphysical destiny materialized in the conscious evolution. This is the fundamental difference between two situations presented to human possibilities.

The spirit is not only the inspirer, the accumulator of energy, the upholder and perpetuator of extra-physical existence, but also the natural linking agent between man and his Creator. Naturally, one should not expect that merely by being informed of this, one would be able to establish this contact, which pertains to a transcendent order. It is logical to presume that one cannot aspire to obtain such a benefit without first having mobilized one's conscience so that the mental "radar" functions without defect.

The indispensable condition for one's spirit to attain such a lofty purpose is to make the behavioral attitudes originated in the soul coincide with the demands of one's spirit, while having disciplined one's self ahead of time in the training conducive to this end.

What does this training consist of? We have already said that the soul integrates the physical entity in its psychological part; consequently, its task is to transform the mind into a kind of a sculptor's workshop and create in the being it sustains the habit, never sufficiently prudent, of watching over and improving thoughts and acts. The first disciplinary readjustments subject to accomplishment through our method, allow the gradual intervention of one's spirit which by taking over the reins of one's life, will promote within the human being an abundance of variations in the way of thinking, of feeling, of observing, of understanding, etc. This is how identification of one's spirit with the physical entity or soul is produced, an identification that culminates in its highest manifestation when man has accomplished all the steps of his self-improvement.

The human spirit does not possess the gift of self-conscious evolution. As a cosmic unit it must perfect itself and become conscious, while it evolves, of the cognitions that exist in Creation. Such an undertaking necessarily requires it to join with the soul or physical entity, a fact that occurs as a result of the magnetic effect of the same hereditary force that attracts them, and the permanent participation of one's conscience. Thereafter, both the spirit and the soul begin their march on the long path towards conscious evolution, culminating, in this journey, the grand experience that will reveal to man the greatest enigma of his existence.

When man elevates his mind above common problems, a vivid radiance surges from his intelligence and is projected over the things that relate to the spirit, familiarizing man with them. A new ability to comprehend and accomplish flows through his mind, and his soul is permeated by a superhuman condition, which implies nothing less than the linkage of his intelligence to the superior world, to the world of great ideas, of elevated thoughts and lofty conceptions of the spirit. It is at this point that man perceives that he is being deified, because in his progressive effort for self-improvement he reaches the privileged regions of the spirit and establishes the first contacts with the universal life, where God's Thought reigns.

Logosophy has repeatedly stated that there is no intermediary between God and man other than man's own spirit, with whom he must connect and to whom he must offer the control of his life. This objective is achieved by enriching one's conscience with transcendent cognition, the only means by which man can understand what his mission is and how his immaterial being is constituted; his own spirit, the agent that responds to the influence of the eternal Universal Conscience, carries with it through the ages the cosmic sign of individual existence.

As a result of what we have said, one will conclude that the spirit, contrary to the hypotheses suggested to this day, is not the soul nor even this superior complex of higher reasonings and inspirations of the mind, whose excellencies neither define nor materialize its existential reality.

We have made a condensed outline of the spirit in order to better materialize the central idea of the individual; an idea which throughout the course of this work, will be complemented in accordance with the various phases and aspects of this singular and profound cognition about the physical and spiritual integration of the human being.

Chapter 9

HOW TO APPROACH AND MAKE CONTACT WITH ONE'S SPIRIT

We suggest to those who are interested in our science that they dedicate themselves to a thorough study of all the circumstances in which the spirit manifests itself totally independent of one's own will and conscience. The analysis will reveal that this manifestation occurs with relative frequency. Later, if this experience repeats itself and if it is not an isolated occurrence, it must deserve, if anything does, the utmost attention on our part.

In no way can we establish a conscious link with the spirit if we begin by ignoring it or refuse to admit that such manifestations represent an unquestionable reality. We must tread on firm ground and in any investigation it is necessary to build a margin of trust not only in the procedure used, but also in the aim pursued, requiring also that we equip ourselves with the necessary dose of circumspection and freedom to be able to address a task of such transcendence.

Because we consider it to be indispensable and in order to convey the unequivocal impression of the seriousness of our statement, we must mention here that prior to consciously approaching and making contact with one's spirit, one must, as vigorously demanded by the high cognition that makes this feasible, achieve the process of conscious evolution which, as we know, is implicitly defined by the knowledge of one's self and of the metaphysical world. It is understood that the task must begin in the individual's inner self, later extending to the cosmos, since in this task are revealed, one by one, the universal laws that govern Creation.

Everyone will easily understand and recognize the logic behind our admonition so that no one will deceive himself by believing that logosophical cognitions could be used as a panacea for instant magical results in this area of investigation, which implies nothing less than to fathom one of the most inscrutable secrets of human existence.

It is obvious that the process of approaching and intimately connecting with one's own spirit requires time and patience, founded upon constant and sincere zeal. If someone claims to have established this connection, we would reply that such a cognition cannot be placed in a back pocket, nor can it be achieved without having first traveled the unique path that leads to it. Man cannot reserve for himself, what is required as an inexcusable duty, to be shared with his fellow men. Up to this moment we are not aware that anyone has addressed this question with the seriousness and precision that we do.

Very reluctantly, we see ourselves compelled to insist in this assertion in order to avoid confusing the clear statements made by the logosophical conception, with those already published, since they differ fundamentally, without even having one small point of coincidence between two such opposing views. As man today and mankind tomorrow develops this new culture, he will evaluate and judge it on its own merits, based on experience, and determine which one contains the truth and which one the error.

Following the course of our dissertation, we wish to cal attention once more to a fact that we consider to be of vital importance to better understand the development of the cognitions that directly or indirectly have a bearing on the subject matter. This fact is the following: that the contacts with one's spirit have been occurring and continue to occur unconsciously, and for that reason its dimensional reality has passed unnoticed, although it is subject to the modifications that occur in its favor in the inner self of each individual. This leads us to think that it is absolutely necessary to establish this contact consciously in order to extract the living essence from the existence that sustains our life since the success of closer ties and identification with it depends on this direct and conscious relationship. Let us not seek its presence outside of ourselves, nor should we pretend to see it through skeptical eyes, because this attitude will lead us nowhere. In order to feel its reality and be in a position to receive the influence of its transparent, and ineffable dictates, we must prepare our psychological and mental structures. The spirit will then be able to make use of them, increasing to a maximum level the possibilities of our mental and sensitive capabilities. When this occurs we will experience the sensation of witnessing a remarkable inner change. Both natures, the spiritual and the physical, end up by merging together following a struggle for the predominance of one over the other.

It is appropriate to indicate which is the best attitude required to initiate the long-awaited correspondence with the incorporeal being with which we are dealing. After the logical preparatory work that we described, one will have to invoke it and communicate with it, in its metaphysical language, the only one it listens to because it is made of the same essence. How is this done? Very simply. It is necessary that we constitute within ourselves a permanent expression of yearnings towards achieving the goal that we set for ourselves, in the same way that we do for other goals in life, without slackening the effort until the first results are obtained. The metaphysical idiom is revealed in the human mind as a result of the knowledge that one obtains from it, proportionate to the familiarization with the terms that are consubstantial to it.

The constant familiarization with the logosophical terminology, which implies penetrating in depth the true context of the words, especially those which contain specific concepts, deeply moves the spirit which is attracted to the area of activity of our intelligence. But, simultaneously, one has to enrich one's conscience by incorporating the cognitions which, like a magnet, attract and absorb those that are in the custody of one's own spirit. In this way, the difficulties that impeded the spirit in the fulfillment of its great and lofty goal, will be overcome.

Let us now refer to a point that we consider to be illustrative and appropriate, which is the error that is involuntarily committed by a majority of human beings when they believe that by enjoying artistic pleasure their spirit is entertained. The same observation applies when man refers to his spirit with such lack of knowledge that he gives the impression of believing that his spirit is always at his beck and call. Gross mistake; one's spirit cannot be that easily attracted after having been ignored throughout one's whole life. Such forgetfulness can only be justified by the individual's ignorance or unconsciousness. This justification, nevertheless, does not even diminish by an iota its consequences, that is, the delay of one's own evolution.

With good reason we affirm that the spirit distrusts the physical being when it intends to attract it into trivial circumstances, since such an endeavor is devoid of any lofty objective in line with the seriousness demanded by one's spirit.

The relationship with one's incorporeal being occurs as a result of a process of mutual familiarization which materializes in each human being according to his individual ability of accomplishment. This occurs in the physical being or soul through the process of conscious evolution, which increases its possibilities and allows it to reach the mental zone of the metaphysical world where the spirit acts; and it occurs in the latter, as it gradually regains the ascension that it lost with the advent of puberty of the physical being.

Logosophical cognitions act as a bridge and simultaneously as a means by which to arrive at this wonderful occurrence which is impossible to achieve by other means. This implies, as we have mentioned, a behavior that is conducive to such an aspiration, in order not to deceive one's own hopes and fall into self-delusion. Determination and constancy in the pursuit of this endeavor to ensure the best results must be maintained steadfastly as an unshakable imperative. In this case, the best course of action is to resort to what logosophically we have denominated as the "authority thought". We are dealing here with a thought that is instituted in the mind, by the will of the individual himself. It is responsible for giving permanency to his aspirations and purposes, ensuring that these overcome any interference that threatens his determination to evolve consciously, in other words, conforming to the logosophical precepts and to the precise exercise of the universal laws. To fix in the authority thought the image that nothing is comparable to this magnificent ascension over each hurdle of human limitations, is of everlasting effects and worthy of a reward infinitely superior to the effort made.

Hence, we can see the mistake made by those who tried to cross over the metaphysical boundaries without the invaluable assistance of their own spirit. The common mind, when managed by the physical entity, will never be able to penetrate the reality of the metaphysical world no matter how high its intellectual development has reached, because it lacks the essential: to know its own spirit and with it to find the ways and means by which to consummate such a lofty aspiration.

Chapter 10

ARTICULATION OF THE HUMAN PSYCHOSPIRITUAL MECHANISM

In the couse of this chapter, one will be able to better appreciate the working of this marvelous psychospiritual structure, which makes man a prominent figure amongst all other living beings.

We must admit, nevertheless, that the fact of being so well-equipped to accomplish his integral self-improvement has not been sufficient to alert man to the fact that he is able to assume such a great and honorable responsibility; and this is proven by him as soon as he decides to embark on the path of conscious evolution which, as it initiates him in the correct use of his psychological mechanism, allows him to assess the benefit that it yields.

For the first time in the history of mankind, man is given the opportunity to explain to himself the existence within him of a mental system, which, once activated through the knowledge of its delicate mechanism, is converted into the symbolic magic key that opens the impenetrable doors that for centuries have been sealed to the requirements of man's reasoning.

Logosophy gives fundamental importance to the human mind, attributing to it transcendental prerogatives. Once educated in a superior culture through the exercise and practice of the cognitions that Logosophy places within its reach, the mind becomes the sovereign instrument of the conscience, with aptitudes that become as fertile as the transcendent cognitions that enlighten it.

It is absolutely necessary to insist on the paramount role that the cognition plays in the exercise of articulating the sublime mechanism of the faculties of the mind, because it is there that the intelligence, in harmony with the cognitions that illustrate it, allows these cognitions to be fixed in the conscience, creating in this manner the transcendent conscience, depository of the cognitions, also transcendent, that enhance the individual hereditary asset.

It is important to note that conscience linked with intelligence, can only manifest itself through the intelligence. On the other hand, conscience receives from and is enriched by the flow of truths which, through the intelligence, reach the individual in the form of cognitions. Certainly the functions of such a valuable yet subtle mechanism escape the attention of the person who does not participate as a conscious executor of the effort that is required, even though we are aware that it would not be difficult to deduce that the conscience uses the intelligence to manifest and enrich itself at the same time, as a result of which the mind becomes as transparent as the conscience itself, responding to the dictates of the latter with an action as fertile as the enlightenment attained by the knowledge acquired.

One must therefore seek a perfect communion between one's mind and one's conscience, because the cognitions deposited in it by one's mind flow back to it as soon as they are needed. This means that the conscience places at the disposal of the mind, now enlightened, the cognitions that the mind contributes to deposit in it. By the same token, the mind is responsive to the conscience by virtue of the interdependent functions that each performs.

The person who decides to undertake such a praiseworthy endeavor cannot ignore the sensitive system since the transcendent cognition regulates the movements of the intelligence and the sensitivity, which explains the importance taken on by the harmonious contact of both systems within the complex inner world of the individual.

We still have to determine the direct correspondence between the spirit and one's conscience which, as mentioned, expands by virtue of the cognitions it absorbs. As it expands, the conscience gives the spirit the opportunity to manifest itself, and not only allows it to receive its influence which continuously urges man to greater effort, but also to experience the broadening of life when it starts to be governed by the spirit.

All life in the universe is moved by the same and unique source of energy. On a smaller scale, man also has inside of him this same source that is activated once it comes into contact with the universal life. This source of energy is the conscience, uniquely capable of moving the whole human psychological mechanism, and with it, the conduits of feeling that make men great, unselfish, and noble.

Chapter 11

OCCURRENCE OF THE SPIRIT IN CHILDHOOD AND ADOLESCENCE

During childhood, the spirit manifests itself in the child's physical being or soul in order to protect him from the evils that threaten him and to share with him very happy moments. We often detect it in the smile on the child's face whether awake or asleep, when it occurs without any apparent motive that justifies it. The fact is that the spirit plays the role of a "granddaddy" and suggests to the child's budding reflection things that, although beyond his comprehension, cause in him an innocent joy. Nonetheless, some things remain etched in the child's mind to reappear later in adulthood as incentives or inspirations that illuminate his journey through the world. There is, however, one more fact that we referred to in previous studies[1] and that we will

[1] See "Mister De Sandara" page 490 by the same author.

now highlight as a revelation since it contains extraordinary values for the present and future orientation of childhood and adolescence. We are referring to the action of the spirit during the period between birth and puberty. During this time, contrary to the current belief that the child's mind is incapable of understanding certain manifestations of adult life and reduces them to mere elementary adaptations of adult concepts, we affirm that the child's mind can grasp and easily understand many of these manifestations, because his own spirit facilitates it.

Logosophy discovers that during this early age human possibilities are amazingly fertile for the natural development of conscious life with all the prerogatives that evolution offers man in the course of his existence. The child's mind is virgin and fertile terrain. It therefore not only constitutes a need but also our inescapable moral and rational obligation to ensure that the best seeds germinate in the small but fertile mental fields of the child, seeds that contain the potential to develop the resources that man's intelligence needs to emancipate himself from any pressure extraneous to his thinking and feeling, and to overcome the difficulties that he will have to face in the course of his life.

We declare as harmful and totally wrong, since it causes great damage to human existence, the fact of inculcating any idea or belief that is contrary to a truth or a reality that a child will be able to prove to himself when he reaches adulthood. The child's mind is extremely sensitive. The images that the elders mold in it as suggestions remain etched in the child's mind in a form that is nearly indelible. This is the case, for example, when fear of God is injected in the child, provoking in him an anguish which is as useless as it is pernicious to his psychological and moral formation, at a time when he has neither yet committed any fault nor does he have any remote idea of what is an offense to moral decency or honor. He is also inculcated with fear of the devil and terrified by so-called "hell". Neither of these two images is constructive and both depress him acutely since, lacking mental defenses, the child is left to the influence of a suggestion that numbs certain areas of his mind, producing the "psychialysis"* which is the paralysis of a part of his mental system, which is precisely

* N.T.: See Initiation Course into Logosophy (paragraph 105) by the same author.

the zone in which his spirit can manifest itself with the aim to govern his life and connect him to the secret of his own inheritance. As may be seen, it is the erroneous intervention of the elders in their function as spiritual tutors, pedagogues or parents aiming at the mental, moral and psychological development of the child that is the cause of the mistakes made by the youth of today, consequently creating a general concern from which nearly no one is exempt. As we consider this cause to be of paramount importance, we present it to the consciousness of all human beings as a means towards the solution demanded and required by such a distressing problem.

It is necessary to foster in children manifestations that protect their spirit, avoiding at all costs anything that would prevent its valuable help. Consequently, one must not etch in their minds any thoughts, ideas, or words that inhibit them or limit their freedom of thinking. Nor should one expose them to depressing moral spectacles in the family or allow them to listen to stories about criminal events, since they are not old enough to understand them. Conversely, one must stimulate in them the love of God, source of all Wisdom; ensure, however, that this love manifests itself as a lofty vocation towards studying and later towards the knowledge of the truths that each one is able to know, that is, to the degree that individual capability allows.

As for love towards parents, brothers and fellow men, this is not a matter of teaching but rather of providing an example. It is on this point, as well as in the error previously stated, where the majority fails. Truly, there are few who through their example inspire this deep love that each child must feel towards his parents. Truly, few older brothers teach their younger brothers by example about the cultivation of affection or mutual respect. And what can we say about the love of one fellow man for another, when one lacks the basic elements of the moral structure needed to maintain a happy relationship.

If the spirit perceives that the being it animates is helped and its evolution favored, if it sees that no ideas or beliefs that it discards as misleading are imposed upon it, the spirit will convert itself into the determining factor of his thinking and feeling, which although still budding in the child, constitutes the strong basis of his mental, moral and spiritual formation, which will grow healthy and broad.

With the above statement we mean to say that the spirit is not born with the human being, but rather it is the immaterial being that is formed throughout the course of our lives according to the extra-physical assets that the individual has been able to accumulate. Such proven wealth contains one's own inheritance, which implies without a shred of a doubt, that the dimension of the spirit's experience and age is greater than that of the physical being it animates, since it carries the sum of the values extracted from each period of the life of the individual entity, be it in this world, be it in the mental or metaphysical world.

We think that we have explained with sufficient clarity the dimensions of this fundamental cognition that reveals the extent that human possibilities can reach and to what degree this has been unknown to those who, had they known it, would have had the duty to teach it to all mankind. The fact of not having done this is proof of their incompetence and a confession of their unsuccessful attempts to go beyond common reflections.

For our part we will penetrate even further into the subject matter to point out some facts that we deem worthy of explanation and are illustrative of the activity of the spirit during the first eleven years of man's physical life.

The direct intervention of the spirit in protecting the lives of children is undeniable. Frequent observations made by us confirm such intervention and the manner in which the spirit exercises its influence over the unconscious movements of children. Many years ago the author of this book was vacationing in a summer resort in his country. Adjacent to his house was an old building with a high frontal entrance, resting upon a massive cornice, displaying huge concrete flower tubs in which abundant weeds proliferated. On the sidewalk next to the building, below a tall concrete tower, three children were playing, the eldest of whom was only seven years old. The house was separated by a fence-like partition made of heavy duty wire that allowed the author to observe the children playing from the garden where he was entertaining a few friends. Suddenly one of the children, probably the eldest, stopped playing and urged his companions to move away from where they were playing. All three had barely taken a few steps when those observing the scene froze in astonishment as they saw the heavy flower tub that minutes before decorated the tall frontal entrance of the building, crash right over the place where the children were playing. To those who observed this event with an open mind there could be no doubt that the child's spirit participated in this, or the spirit of all three considering that the impulse to move away was practically unanimous.

Here is another testimony: Some time ago an eight-year-old child was walking on the railroad tracks at a time when a passenger train was advancing at high speed. Absorbed in his world, the child was unaware of what was happening and, due to the noise of the roaring vehicle, he was unable to hear the screams of those who were warning him of the danger. At a given moment, a providential stumble hurled him away out of reach of the terrible machine thus avoiding his being sucked into the air turbulence of the wagons in their soaring course. What caused him to stumble? What saved the child from a painful end to his budding life? It can only and uniquely be his own spirit, the sublime expression of the supreme foresight that protects in this manner every human child during the period of total unconsciousness to the dangers that threaten him, and to those who are exposed to this uncertain period of human life.

We could cite countless similar cases to which we would have to add those that the reader undoubtedly retains in his memory as observations or as events which he has experienced. Nevertheless, the cases cited suffice to form a judgment on the evidence with which the spirit manifests itself protecting the being it animates. To attribute this to other causes or factors would be to step onto the slippery ground of presumptions that only lead to remaining indefinitely ignorant with regard to a reality whose value is of paramount importance to the development of the moral and mental aptitudes of the individual and which has contributed so much to elevate life and endow it with a spiritual content of unsuspected significance.

One will ask, however, why is it that so many children die in accidents every day? Where is the protection of the spirit in these cases? The answer to these logical questions does not destroy our statement since all lives do not follow the same course nor are they influenced by the same factors. The laws that bestow upon us freedom of our actions are the ones that later determine the pros and cons which are manifested throughout our existence. Let us not forget therefore that the life of a child could be conditioned to the verdict of the laws regarding the evolutionary development of his parents or of himself. Additionally, should not one recognize that the consequences generated by the lack of foresight and carelessness which are often the causes of painful accidents in children, are also part of life's hard experiences?

Following the order of this exposition which is the result of thorough investigation coupled with the implementation of the logosophical cognitions that penetrate deep into the complex articulations of the human psychology, we will now point to an event that occurs in all souls once puberty is reached. The awakening of this critical age brings with it the withdrawal of the spirit. It is precisely at this age, in which the needs regarding precise notions of the spirit are most pressing, when the individual is found lacking in all illustrative explanation, when not misinformed with ambiguous and confused interpretations often given by the elders. We should remember, nevertheless, that these elders in their time received in turn from others similar erroneous concepts.

With the advent of adolescence, the self-imposed

withdrawal of the spirit is due to the fact that at that age the instinct strengthens, passion surges and the physical being finds himself suddenly submerged in the crudest materialism. Here, we must point out a fact that is repeated countless times: that under such circumstances, the spirit suffers an eclipse that in many cases becomes permanent. In fact, one cannot even detect traces of its existence in the thoughts, ideas or acts of an infinite number of human beings whose lives terminate in an irreparable descent.

Let us now see how one can neutralize the strength of the instinct during puberty and avoid the annulment of the spirit's influence. In the experimental field of logosophical activities it has been proven that the special attention accorded to children with the use of the logosophical method allows them to enter puberty without being overtaken by fears, inhibitions, and the whole array of suggestions which arise simultaneously with the awakening of sex. It is precisely in these circumstances that the dark images that were inculcated in him during childhood surface in the mind and feelings of the adolescent. The fear of God enslaves and oppresses him not allowing him to reflect upon his own difficulties. Hounded by such thoughts, he feels just short of being an offender of the natural laws. Generally, this leads him to imprudent actions and errors, which, each time more intensively weaken his moral shield. Logosophy has foreseen this disturbing situation which the adolescent is subjected to, because he lacks the resources to face up to the inevitable change that occurs between one age and the other. It teaches him to create his own mental defenses and guides him to get to gradually know the contingencies he will have to face so that he can resolve them naturally by means of a serene reflection about the facts. In this manner, one is able to have the spirit maintain its influence over the individual as it did during his childhood; and it is in the mental and psychic force that it conveys to him that the adolescent finds his leverage point to avoid going astray during that delicate test of his existence on earth.

In the logosophical home, morals naturally contribute decisively in building in the children and the adolescents an unequivocal idea of life's development in its most prudent and sensible terms. The power of providing an example at home allows them to verify later what occurs in non-logosophical environments and to judge for themselves the benefits of each one being, the master of his thoughts and actions. In this manner, they seek the pattern of morals to deploy the inner energies that one's own individual spirit knows quite well how| to use, overcoming without much difficulty the alternatives that this critical period of life presents.

It will be understood that when the adolescent is deprived of the mental defenses which Logosophy teaches him to organize, he is compelled to sustain painful struggles between his thinking and feeling. Most of these struggles visibly affect his health and shake up his morals. With these disadvantages which are the result of ignorance and inexperience, he passes from puberty into life. The new concerns he faces will gradually restore in him the functional balance of his inner occurrences, but as he walks through the paths of the world lacking a clear orientation, he will quickly be trapped by new attacks of the instinct and the nonetheless impetuous assaults of certain thoughts, which, entrenched in his mind, seek to seize control of his life.

When one considers in all serenity the serious risks conveyed to the human being as a result of a neglected childhood and youth, one can easily assess the importance of protecting the child, at a very early age, from prejudices, beliefs, and any other suggestive and inhibiting idea that threatens the normal development of his thinking nature and of other attributes related to his condition of superiority above all other creatures. The child will then exit from his world, the world of childhood, to enter the world of adolescence, equipped with defenses against the contaminations that threaten him while receiving, moreover, the assistance of his elders who are responsible for making him aware of the perspectives of a life which for him has suddenly changed. Most frequently, however, we do see the adolescent abandoned, with no recourse other than the illusions that surge abundantly from his imagination as a result of the accumulation of new and varied manifestations experienced by his nature. We should remember, nevertheless, the many cases in which an unexpected idea, or a healthy reaction in the very moment of taking a wrong step, enables us to observe that the favorable and innocent influences of the early state of existence have not totally disappeared, remaining undoubtedly as reminiscences that the Universal Wisdom uses in protect the incipient explorer as he blindly penetrates this complicated world of the great human experience.

Logosophy has pointed out the path to man by revealing to his understanding the possibilities he possesses to reunite with his spirit and to experience consciously the reality of his existence. It is preferable and highly beneficial for the soul to master the scope of its possibilities rather than continuing to ignore them. The twinkling of a light in the darkness of night can serve as a beacon when we are overtaken by darkness in the wide plains; but we must depend on our own strength to reach the light. The expert does not need the twinkle because he carries within himself the precise orientation to avoid getting lost.

Chapter 12

SOMETHING IMPORTANT RELATIVE TO INHERITANCE WHICH ALSO HAS TO DO WITH MAN'S DESTINY

The observations and verifications made as a result of logosophical investigation have established that the spirit gathers and keeps from the being it animates those substantial assets which integrate the estate of one's own inheritance. It is sad, however, to admit that in the great majority of human beings these assets are practically non-existent due to having lived in deplorable spiritual poverty. It becomes apparent how few were able to increase such valuable wealth and if they did, it was done without being truly conscious of it. Our assertion in the case of child prodigies, which is exempt from any mystery, emerges and becomes evident in this human reality that was never explained satisfactorily.

We have already stated that the spirit protects and inhabits, so to speak, the physical being during the years of childhood. Well then, when by impulse of one's own inheritance, the premature awakening of a faculty, such as that of memory, is exceptionally produced, then the spirit itself uses it to connect it to the knowledge that accumulated in that inheritance. When this faculty is enhanced to the limit of its previous achievement, one can observe the marvelous coordination of both natures acting in concert although the child has absolutely no consciousness of what is happening to him, since he is extraneous to the process leading to the premature development of this faculty. The prodigy usually disappears with the first manifestations of puberty, due to the influence of the instinct at that age. There are cases, however, in which the influence of the spirit is extended through an inclination or vocation that coincides with a similar one that occurred in past epochs. Here, the reminiscence takes on the full strength of its; reality and in an aesthetic rebirth, transcends the age of forget fullness during puberty and finds itself blooming during youth. Similar cases can be observed in the ease with which many people practice a profession or master a certain field of human activity. Therefore, it becomes quite clear to the wise and skillful observer of such investigations, how those people demonstrate in an unobjectionable form the benefit of self-inheritance[1], even though not conscious of it, a conception that we covered in one of our previous books.

Such affirmation rests on the fact that men who are endowed with an illustrious intelligence and distinguish themselves in one field or another, be it in science or in art, although favored by such inheritance do not always display characteristics of equal hierarchy where moral and spiritual values are concerned. Many are those who do not demonstrate a degree of inner refinement in accordance with their geniality. The imbalance caused by the unilateral exaltation of the faculties is well known, as is the case when they delight the individual to the point of inebriation and end up by erasing any other noble possibility in his nature. In such cases it would seem that the hand of the Creator is warning us that life must be exalted in all it manifestations.

[1] See "Self-Inheritance" by the same author

The assets made available to us by the spirit in the advanced stage of conscious evolution, do not produce imbalances, but rather favor the harmonization of all the faculties that constitute the human psychology, which help to distinguish oneself in determined areas of the intelligence. Logosophy teaches man to become conscious of the assets inherited from the spirit and to make the best use of them in favor of his evolution. As can be seen, this fact is of decisive importance to the destiny that each one forges for his own good.

Despite what has just been explained regarding the activity of one's own incorporeal being, which exercises such a fundamental mission in the destiny of our existence, we shall point out some episodes that will explain the reasons why some events have not acted in accord with the knowledge or the will of the individual. It has been said, for instance, since antiquity, and sustained to this very day – although no more than as a poetic figure of speech – that artists receive their inspired impulses from certain deities, the Muses, or from a generic power named Divinity. Beautiful illusion! But a thousand times more beautiful and real is to know now, concretely, that it is one's own spirit which extracts from one's hereditary assets the mental elixir that makes possible the work of art, the musical creation, or the poetic ecstasy; to also know that it is one's own spirit which makes possible one's heroic and unselfish deeds whether on the field of battle or science. Surely, such gestures do not occur as a result of abstract inspirations, but to precise manifestations of the spirit of its protagonists.

This hereditary asset, heretofore unsuspected, may be compared to the funds that we frequently deposit in a bank, and that at a certain moment we withdraw in order to increase their value through some commercial or financial operation. Consequently, these constitute our own reserves. Hence, therefore, he who has not during any stage of physical life dedicated his efforts towards a specific preference – art for example – and at a given moment it occurs to him to dedicate himself to it, in vain will he claim the assistance of his spirit because no funds at all have been deposited in this "bank account", and obviously the so-called "divinity" will not able to inspire him.

One should not think, however, that the assistance of the spirit which we referred to, has anything to do with the process of conscious evolution that Logosophy teaches us to accomplish. No, we mention it with the objective of showing, on one hand, how these manifestations occur outside the individual's awareness and will; and on the other, to point out the error attributing to them an unreality, a sterile figure to the human life.

Certainly, it is totally different when the physical being guided by these cognitions, dedicates his life to the highest and most extraordinary of all the arts, which is to shape his own sculpture, molding it in accomplishments of the highest and loftiest transcendent value, or be it the work of individual betterment, which implicitly brings with it the immortal breath of Wisdom. This work could never be executed unless the systems that constitute the human psychology are adequately prepared beforehand and more so if a continuous upkeep of the conscious state is not maintained, since the conscience must not be alien to any volitive movement made towards this goal.

We have to mention another important point here: the opportunity that we offer our own spirit to gather and conserve all the valuable content of our life as it relates to the superior achievement made in each of the favorable events that our conscious evolution determines. We are referring to self-inheritance, that is, to everything that we are able to become and possess in wisdom in proportion to the mental capability reached within the spheres of the metaphysical world. Logosophy has defined this world as the cosmic environment wherein the universal laws in their multiple configurations and effects act. For this reason, embracing the dimension of such knowledge will always depend upon the effort of the individual, upon the determination exercised by each one in the consummation of the process of one's conscious evolution. We have to point out, however, that those who follow the logosophical disciplines are given effective assistance by those who are most advanced in the studies of this science, assistance that is of an inestimable value in clearly defining the behavior that must be followed in each circumstance, in order to achieve through study and inner accomplishment, full control over each logosophical cognition.

We must not forget that the advent of one's own spirit is an event that implies a rebirth and a permanent essential modification of life, and as such, of one's own destiny. Anyone who does not understand this before the fact occurs and thinks that he could continue in the same routine and common expressions of his current way of life would be better off to remain outside the scope of this superior reality that we are presenting to his reasoning and feeling. No one who has lived in captivity can behave, once free, as he was obliged to when he was enslaved. Thus, in a similar manner, he who yearns to extend the control of his intelligence to superior levels of the conscience, once this objective is reached, cannot behave thereafter as if this event had not occurred. Therefore, it will be one's own spirit which will demand from the being it animates, and in exchange for its invaluable contribution, a behavior harmony with the new way of thinking, feeling, and acting and this behavior can only be in complete synergy with the level of his investigations, and without being subject to the interferences of those thoughts[2] which acted before he penetrated, albeit initially, into the grand enigma of his own existence.

We have clearly explained that the essential function of spirit is to perpetuate itself throughout existence; and since this perpetuation must necessarily

[2] See "Logosophy Science and Method" (Lesson IV) by the same author.

have a cause that activates it, this cause is defined by the conscious evolution which, in turn, determines the course of one's own inheritance until it culminates in the inexpressible heights of possessing Wisdom. This is the reason why the spirit feels irresistibly attracted when the soul decisively undertakes the process of conscious evolution, because it is there, in the conscience, where the sublime conciliation between the spirit and the physical being or soul takes place. Naturally, this can only happen after constant training of the mental and sensitive articulations which equips them for that purpose. One will have to extricate from the mind every thought opposed to that objective and favor to a maximum degree the flow of those other thoughts that contribute in the development of said process. We repeat here once again the importance of having an authority thought whose governing function is to impose the necessary discipline over our will, over our thoughts and actions, in order to avoid on one hand sterile impediments to our efforts, and on the other, to foster the invaluable contribution that our spirit will make.

Therefore, we leave it to the reader to assess the values of a cognition that leads man to the encounter with his spirit, in order to receive from its hands the wealth of his inheritance. He will further be able to recognize the expression of justice revealed in the great law of evolution that establishes for all intelligent creatures who inhabit the earth the same unyielding conscious conduct for ascending the steps of Universal Wisdom. It should be understood from the above that if the individual's hereditary assets are not satisfactory, in as much as it is one's self which is solely responsible, there remains the possibility of enriching it and enjoying even today its magnificent rewarding virtue. Logosophy provides everything to those who have not, as well as to those who have, or believe they have, as much as is needed to allow them to discover their truth and be happy.

Chapter 13

THE UNIVERSAL LAWS

Having revealed the factors which intervene in the daily occurrences of each individual's inner world, Logosophy places within man's reach the key to the causal knowledge of his life, evolution, and destiny. Universal laws cannot remain indifferent to such prerogatives, since they sustain the pillars of Creation and bestow life to everything that exists. Man's duty is to avoid infringing upon them and favor at all times the integrity of their designs by complying with their mandates, which give him the absolute assurance of their protection.

The laws upon which official science bases its investigations and discoveries emerged from the need to organize that which relates to the material behavior or physical activity of the human biological

CARLOS BERNARDO GONZÁLEZ PECOTCHE (RAUMSOL)

organism, and of all kinds of processes included in nature, which are subject to proof. No mention is made to us of the conscious prerogatives of man, nor of the evolution of his possibilities of reaching the high spheres of the spirit.

The tasks of the universal laws which Logosophy teaches are identified with norms of a superior ethic, in synergy with its nature, and its orientation coincides with the venue of cognitions of a superior order that the logosopher cultivates. Said laws establish a new relation of cause and effect that is conductive to easily understanding the broad panorama of human existence, while orienting and prescribing norms of conduct necessary to cover the successive stages of self-improvement.

We must admit that the laws of Creation are still barely known by mankind, and since they act simultaneously as attorneys and judges, most people ignore how they work and how they pass their sentences after judgment. By ignoring this, man is unable to know the facts of his inner life, which are capable of exceeding his most fantastic lucubrations every time a law expresses itself in harmony with the other laws.

When Logosophy enlightens man as to the mechanism of universal laws, it allows him to adjust his life to the reality established by them, freeing him from the emptiness and moral oppression caused by the lack of knowledge of these laws. Hence, he begins to control the area closest to him in which these laws act, be it precisely the area that each one occupies, that is one's own life, the human being's life, and as a result of the knowledge he accumulates, he also learns that everything in the universe is accomplished through processes.

In shaping the image of the human creature, God bestowed upon it the ability to comply with all the evolutionary cycles regulated by the supreme laws. Logically, therefore, by knowing the laws and improving everything in himself that is subject to improvement, man will gradually understand what his destiny and conduct must be.

Cosmic processes, which are governed by the immutable laws that regulate life throughout the entire universe, set the norm for all other processes that are carried out in it, including the human process, which makes it easy to understand why they hand down sanctions for any deviation or fault made.

Man establishes contact with universal laws by means of the conscience; therefore, it is imperative to highlight the importance of this valuable linking factor by strengthening the purpose of not infringing upon them, all of which greatly favors the process of conscious evolution. At this point, errors will not be committed and liabilities will be avoided; we will not, therefore, attract any sanctions.

Everything in nature is governed by a universal norm; a norm that corrects the offenders. In civilian life people are fined or arrested so that they become aware of their errors and avoid repeating them; in the transcendental world it is exactly the same except that instead of depriving people of their freedom or fining them, the laws correct them asking them to understand by different means that they must not disobey them.

Human law has been inspired by universal laws and tends to be similar to them, although they are far from perfect, since the universal laws besides being absolutely fair, fulfill their mandate with rigorous accuracy and punctuality; human law contains gross flaws, most of which originate in men's own weaknesses.

We must accustom ourselves to thinking that the laws are eminently fair in passing judgment on our acts. If we receive an adverse judgment, we should never think that in our sorrow lies the punishment, but rather the opportunity of paying off a debt, of freeing ourselves from something negative that still persists. This will require us to consider the action of the laws from a humanitarian point of view, allowing for a better understanding of their mechanism and the generosity with which they act.

God, the only being in Creation who has no equal, descends to man by virtue of His Laws and His Thought, expressed in every one of the things that is created. With the prerogative of being able to become in spirit similar to Him, man was granted the prerogative of knowing his laws in order to let them govern his life as a human being and immortalize his existence as a spiritual being.

Chapter 14

THE INHERITANCE GATHERED BY THE SPIRIT AND CARRIED AWAY AS A BURDEN OR AS AN OVERWHELMING DEBT

Notwithstanding its immaterial nature, exempt from any terrestrial contamination, the spirit absorbs from the physical being to which it is bound – that which is positive, as we previously explained – as well as all that is negatively represented by the crimes, mistakes, and transgressions committed during life, covering a wide range from the most inhuman cruelties down to the slightest faults.

Universal laws are inexorable; nothing and no one escapes their sphere of influence. Therefore, where man is concerned, it becomes also inexorable that the law governs his inheritance. To the latter, thrones, academic titles and golden robes are worthless if the thoughts and the will of those who used such tokens gave origin to one's own misfortune and to the misfortune of one's fellow man. In such cases, black papers integrate the book of individual inheritance, the same applying to all those who, with identical results and whatever having been their activity in the physical life, have enjoyed a position at the moral and material expense of their fellow man. No spirit is, therefore, exempt from this task, so wisely established by the Supreme Maker. This implies that each one is directly responsible for his destiny; that upon each one rests an exclusive responsibility for his survival and perpetuation as an individual who either lifts himself towards the extra physical heights where God's Cosmic Thought reigns, or disappears absorbed and disintegrated by the inertia that originated his deviations. Man can still detain the annulment of his spiritual being if he makes use of the great opportunity granted to him as an expression of the highest level of justice by that same law of self-inheritance that allows him to free himself and become his own self-redeemer.

It now remains to be seen in what way he will have to redeem himself. Logosophy makes this sublime realization of the inner life possible by teaching man to wash his faults with the purified water that emanates from the individual inner sources as soon as he decides to conduct his life in the path of the personal conscious experience, that is to say, when, by his own will, he gradually begins to repair all the evil he may have caused during his long pilgrimage in the world. But we insist on asking: "How will this be done? How to relieve the soul from the overwhelming burden of its faults?" Logosophy answers with the absolute assurance that characterizes its pronouncements. Not only does it respond affirmatively, but it also teaches how to achieve it.

As long as man is not conscious of the fact that he is able to repair his faults, he will incessantly repeat them due to the lack of knowledge about his capability to redeem himself. When he becomes conscious of this reality and realizes that only he, and he alone, can erase them through reparatory actions that exceed their dimension, he will experience the inexpressible happiness of feeling free from the deception he was subjected to, believing that someone else could redeem him in his place. If you threw stones at your house, you would break the glass and damage it; if you allowed your fields to be covered by weeds such negligence would not be rectified by imploring help from Providence or trusting that someone would descend from the sky to clean them up. No, this would never happen, because it goes against the same law that establishes man's line of conduct and evolution. Nor would it be honest or sensible to expect others to repair the damage caused by us.

It should be understood on the other hand that God cannot feel pity towards the emotional act of a person who expresses his repentance for the errors he has been committing. Once one institutes in himself the process of conscious evolution, it behooves him to judge himself. Therefore, he cannot pass on to anyone else the act of feeling sorry or dismayed for the situation created. If God were to admit man's repentance as sufficient justification to absolve him, the very laws created by Him would prohibit it immediately.

The repentance that one invokes during an emotional moment does not in any way represent evidence that the person is truly repentant. The emotional feeling produced by the confession of his errors, sincere as it may be, is nothing more than a promise. Repentance by itself does not eliminate the cause of the damage; even when it is deeply felt, it could disappear from the conscience before the error is verified. How then can absolution be expected if one's constancy in the sincerity of purpose has not been proven? This evidently implies that the purpose of amendment must last until it is accomplished; one should demonstrate with facts the understanding of the error and pledge to correct it by eliminating the causes that originated it, or, as we said previously, by exercising goodness of a greater dimension than that of the error made. In other words, the purpose to amend must be made clearly evident by the performance of meritorious acts. This is the means of achieving true pardon; a pardon that elevates human morals and is handed down by a court that passes sentence from within one's inner self.

Every time we actively intervene to rehabilitate ourselves for our own sake, neutralizing our prejudices with the necessary understanding of the error, instantly we reap a significant result from such a positive experience. If our error harms a fellow being, and if for some reason we are unable to correct it with a deed that benefits him, we should then do good to others – the more the better – knowing with certainty that we have made recompense. To act any other way implies fomenting the blind development of the instinct towards evil, this terrible scourge of one's inner self that extinguishes the light of understanding and makes one relapse into error. The faster the spirit is rid of the burden it carries, the sooner it will be ready to give its invaluable assistance to the physical being.

We must point out something of great importance here that will have to be considered by our readers and by those who are disposed to try out our method[1] in order to experience for themselves the truth mentioned. Goodness must be exercised consciously, with full knowledge of why it is done; and that in all cases it must have an altruistic and truly generous end. If we do good to somebody, we must ensure beforehand that this good will not die in him, since by offering it to a selfish person it will inevitably lose its volume and its humanitarian expression. However, if we make that person understand that our thoughts are meant to arouse

[1] See "Logosophy Science and Method" (Lesson VIII) by the same author.

in him the need to help others, who may be as needy or more so than he is, we will then have preserved our goodness from being a sure loss. The person who has been helped will not be able to ask for our assistance any more if we observe that his behavior thereafter was not altered by the advice given to him at the time.

We should also add that the spirit, which is immaculate, seeks only one thing: goodness. Man has always sought the same thing by virtue of the undeniable influence of his spirit. Why not, therefore, create goodness in one's self? Could we expect to find it, or deserve it, by the mere fact of having sought it? These two questions should be addressed by those who are dedicated to this search. Yet, a third question may be in order. How can goodness be created?

First, we should be aware that for Logosophy to be good, or to be better, means to be more conscious. This is the only way one can be good in the broad sense of the word. If it were not, then kindness, the kindness that is not born in one's conscience, can be dangerous; at a given moment it can change to something that is not kindness. Consequently, he who decides to create goodness in his inner domain will begin by creating in it small good deeds. The sum of those small deeds over time will gradually turn into a greater good, in the same way as he who saves every day a small sum of money will see it accumulate and finally amount to a considerable capital. In compliance with that same law of heredity, goodness will continue to expand its volume within each one until it signals that an undeniable capability has been born in us, a capability not only to do good generously, but to do it knowingly. All these good deeds united become more valuable than the material deeds, because they last through eras and centuries, as a small creation within the Great Creation. It is, therefore, within man's possibility to give life to a small creation, modest, but eternal like Creation, because he would have integrated within himself particles extracted from it.

Many of the methods used up to now to address the evils that hurt the human creature will have to change in due time, and this will occur undoubtedly in accordance with our affirmation, considering that the most serious evils that burden man are ignorance and unconsciousness. From these evils emanate everything man does to the detriment of his own being, as they continually predispose him towards deviation and wrongdoing. It is imperative, therefore, to eliminate one or more of these causes so as not to have to experience the prior struggles between his two natures, because while he concentrates his strength towards the elimination of the evils that harm him, he will also broaden his conscience with the acquired cognitions, all of which generate the happiness of becoming the conscious witness of his own life.

Chapter 15

GOD'S HELP REACHES MAN
UNIQUELY BY WAY OF THE SPIRIT

In this moments of pain, of great moral or physical suffering, when man, broken, cries out for help from above, it does not occur to him to think that it is precisely the spirit that gives him the encouragement and the consolation he so urgently needs.

Man usually invokes God, unaware that even when his request is granted, He will deliver His help only by way of this singular agent of ours, the spirit, which is uniquely qualified to protect man in moments of extreme hardship. We cannot sensibly admit that God, who attends to all the processes of creation, wherein evolve countless millions of suns, planets and worlds subject to his absolute rule, can be distracted even for a moment to assist one creature or another among the many that beseech His divine help in the immensity of the cosmos.

In addition to the above, it would be important to remember the statement we have so frequently affirmed: that human beings invoke God in their moments of misfortune expecting immediate protection, unaware, however, that few invoke Him as an homage of gratitude for their moments of happiness, and fewer still to show Him the result of their efforts to connect with His magnificent Will etched in Creation. It is necessary, therefore, to remember Him also during the moments of joy; such recollection not only makes it lose its speculative character, but surges from the gratitude towards the happiness of living. In such cases, then surely the individual spirit can elevate the soul and connect it to superior vibrations.

If one did not have a precise notion of the spirit's true values, it would not be possible to understand the extent and dimension of the assistance it can give us. If we deny it because we do not recognize its objective and real existence, we would be hindering any action it might take in our favor. However, if we prepare our mental and sensitive systems by adequately organizing them, we would offer it excellent opportunities to manifest itself, more so because of its own needs than the needs of our physical being. In this manner, we will be able to acknowledge the benefits bestowed by the spirit as the direct agent between the Creator and man during the long journey that leads to Him.

Although we have already made reference to it in previous chapters, we would be remiss if we did not repeat that man must set lofty objectives for himself and favor uninterruptedly his progress towards the self betterment of his inner state, which not only allows for the free expansion of the spirit, but converts man into the heir of the values that the Supreme Will reserved for him.

Chapter 16

THE AUTONOMY OF THE SPIRIT

The spirit enjoys absolute autonomy in as much as it is of eternal essence and exists without the particular limitations of human nature. This should lead every man who seeks knowledge to reflect and value in its true importance the enormous advantage obtained by his linkage and identification with his spirit.

Nobody will deny that the spirit has remained an extraneous being to his person by not giving him a moment of active participation in the deeds of his life. Nonetheless, as we said in another chapter, the spirit has never ceased to goad the physical being with anxiety, inciting him to the search in spite of the resistances, indecisions and excuses that have occurred in his life, and maintaining it in constant oscillation, while time runs inexorably, thus making the journey more and more painful.

The message Logosophy brings to man is defined in the objective of making him understand that his existence is permanently out of touch with his spirit which, consequently, limits him to enjoy only his "personal experience" during the brief lapse of his physical existence. He cannot make use of the grand experience amassed by his spirit since this is only possible through the process of conscious evolution.

When man seeks opportunities that illuminate his intelligence with the light of knowledge, and his sensitivity displays the sublime manifestations peculiar to it, his spirit will assist him and preside over all the deeds of his life. This life will therefore take on characteristics that will distinguish it from the one lived previously. It will contain optimism, energy and noble yearnings.

We will never insist enough on the extraordinary influence exercised by the process of conscious evolution on our life as it restores to the human being, who is often a victim of distortions which disfigure his temperament, a praiseworthy degree of psychological balance. As long as the human being thinks, by intimately relating his thought to his consciousness, the spirit will breathe freely in his life, and will expand and share the alternatives presented to him. It is usually the physical being or soul which faces the harshness, sometimes extremely demanding, of the daily struggles. How many people have succumbed and how many others live embittered subjected to the burden of such situations? Why? Precisely because the human being fights alone without the direct assistance of the spirit. Logosophy has often proven that when the physical being favors the company of the spirit, when he seeks it, man triumphs, conquers the obstacles, overcomes the difficulties and knows how to endow his life with dignity, with purity and greatness of soul.

The spirit's autonomy will appear more clearly if we added to what was stated above that the spirit is neither subjected to nor dependent on the physical being. On the contrary, it is the physical being that must submit to its influence and be prepared to receive from the spirit's hands the invaluable contribution of his heritage. This contribution, which the spirit rigorously safeguards, is dispensed to man in parts and only after proven demonstrations of efficiency; this means that it is the spirit that disposes and not the individual, inasmuch as it depends upon the former's wish to completely submit to the requirements of the latter. It should be understood that as the spirit is the great agent created by God to animate and activate the physical being, its intervention is regulated by the physical being's progress in the path of conscious evolution, which by fostering the spirit's impulse allows it to measure the dose of the individual heritage, delivering it to man in proportion to his progress. In this manner, the spirit gives evidence of its autonomy expressed in what it retains and grants.

As an autonomous entity and in spite of being kept at a distance imposed by the soul as a result of its human ignorance, the spirit maintains itself agile and always vigilant, ready to intervene in any particular circumstance and find solutions to extreme problems that occur in man's life. The spirit is extremely swift; it instantly conceives and determines what is or is not convenient to do.

The autonomy of the spirit is likewise proven by a series of events that confirm it[1].For example: faced

[1] See "The Mechanism of Conscious Life" (Chapter X) by the same author.

with a pressing problem, a man desperately seeks a happy solution and does not find it. It so happens, however, that after a night of tiring insomnia, he awakens and suddenly finds the means to resolve it. What managed his intelligence when, with his senses asleep, the control of his faculties stopped? Therefore, it was his spirit that intervened and brought forth the solution which, during the vigil, the physical being was incapable of finding. To deny this reality would be like sealing the doors that give access to a new world in which human possibilities take on an unusual transcendence and thereafter forego the assistance given by this extraordinary agent which, although integrating our being and our life, remains ignored by those who could greatly benefit from its extremely efficient help. We are referring to the common man for whom nothing exists inside or outside of his person other than his body which he adores so much, and the aforementioned "me" in which he encloses all his egotism and concentrates his greatest hopes.

The preceding example illustrates the manner by which the spirit takes advantage of moments when the physical being is asleep, in order to use the mind and the thoughts that inhabit it, allowing the physical being, on frequent occasions, to remember, once he awakens, the solution he sought in vain during his vigil.

Among many other facts that reveal to us the isolated action of the spirit, let us take the case of a man disposed to commit suicide, who must unexpectedly attend a funeral. Observing the corpse, he saw himself after the suicide; the fact impressed him so deeply that for the first time he granted life its approximate value and understood that he would not waste it, that life is a great school to which one comes to learn and accomplish lessons of the most transcendental nature. Does not this fact reveal the authority of a force acting outside of a mind overcome by depression and pain? Could it be other than the spirit which acted swiftly here?

It is undoubtedly the spirit that encourages life and sustains it when man must endure the bitter moments of his existence. Let us not be misled that it could be something else, or discard such a reality, because this would erect a huge barrier in the path which would impede our ascent to the spheres of the spirit in the plenitude of our conscience.

We can observe, for instance, that when we find ourselves in a paroxysm of pain or suffering that goes beyond our ability to endure, our physical and moral resistance give way as though our reserves were exhausted. It is during these moments that one usually feels and experiences the unexpected assistance of something astonishing. An unknown inner force encourages and comforts us by sustaining and reassuring our inner state of mind. What caused this force to surface, soothe our pain, and expel from the mind the dark thoughts that fueled our sorrow? We repeat: nobody should be deceived any longer by attributing this to extraneous factors; as ponderable as these may be they will always be extraneous to our reality, and as such, irreconcilable with our reason for being, thinking, and feeling. It is the spirit consequently which, in addition to perpetuating the essence of our existence as previously mentioned, instills in us during crucial circumstances the extra physical value that only it can instill. How much sweetness then spills over life, how much strength emerges from within, if not to resolve the difficulty, at least to face up to it with determination. And the spirit has never refused to share the pain of the physical being, above all when the latter invokes it with his thought. We should, therefore, revere it by keeping in our innermost being the respect we owe it. This will break the spell of so much superstition that for centuries and millenniums has prevented human beings from overcoming their setbacks and it will allow them to awaken into a world that can only be reached through one's own spirit.

We would now like to clarify a matter of great importance: the spirit does not always manifest itself in the manner described. In many cases it abstains from intervening because it knows that certain suffering is the direct result of repeated errors and faults on the part of the person who is suffering. In this case, the suffering acts as a purifying filter, which does not discharge the debt from the person who caused it, since no process at all was followed by him to understand the issue. In other words, while pain purifies the soul from repeated contamination, man's moral debt to his own spirit subsists.

Chapter 17

THE DISINTEGRATION
OF THE SPIRIT BY INERTIA

It is important to emphasize order to eliminate any shred of doubt that even though the individual spirit is the depository of all the evil done by the being it animates, as it is also for the good, its nature is not contaminated, but the heavy burden of its faults gradually immobilizes it until it succumbs to inertia; this occurs when its capacity for resistance has been exhausted. This truly is the second death, the final one[1].

[1] In spite of the great prerogative that man has to perpetuate himself through inheritance, a fact that is defined and expressed in the superior formation of the conscience, in other words when the soul reaches its true objectives of a permanent evolutionary action, this perpetuation will not be fulfilled if the laws are deceived or if the precepts that determine the progress towards such objectives are infringed upon. "The individual inheritance can suffer relaxation and this relaxation may even bring about its dissolution as the line that individualizes man within his species. The cause of this lies in the logical depuration that the Law of Inheritance carries out through the channels of selection, since it would be of scant interest to the purposes of human evolution to effect the perpetuation of a man, for example, who has

We will penetrate a little deeper into the subject so that our word reaches the reader with more clarity. One must understand that by the disintegration of the spirit we mean the final disconnection between the latter and the individual conscience, which, as was mentioned, absorbs the balance of the values distilled from the positive and the negative experiences as well as from the cognitions acquired.

The perpetuation of the spirit is only concerned with intra-individual positive aspects or, in logosophical terms, the sum of the acquired superior cognitions and of the good deeds achieved with these cognitions during the different stages of one's existence; to be even more specific, it is the essence of the thoughts that presided over each life's stages and gave each one an exemplary content.

shown, in all the stages of his life, the signs, expressions and characteristics of a barbarian, or of an individual who, in his decadence, has fallen far below the limits permitted by this law." ("Self-Inheritance", by the same author).

The inertia that affects the needs of one's inner life in which the spirit makes its repeated demands by means of multiple manifestations, postpones the formation of the individual conscience. This inertia can become chronic and permanent, condemning the spirit to permanent immobility. In this case its presence in the being would already have no purpose, since the spiritual heritage, that is, self-inheritance, would have passed from paralysis to dissolution, and the individuality, condensed in this heritage, succumbs through inertia. The spirit then returns to its world, the metaphysical, to animate another being, another movement and another life. The individual spirit, therefore, disintegrates, that is, gone are the sum of the internal traits that differentiate one man from the other.

The incorruptible and eternal essence of Creation maintains the secret of its perpetuity in constant renewal. The law of conservation therefore governs all that renews itself, that changes and improves through continuous activity. Man was given this prerogative by the law of evolution, which means, changing his state of mind, by moving from the inferior to the superior, achieving progressively higher degrees of conscience. A change of mind implies preparing the mind and the soul to enable them to reach the luminous contacts with the metaphysical world. In this constant work of self-improvement the individual gradually eliminates from himself, as a result of the renewal and the uprooting of old tendencies, the absurd beliefs and concepts of an evident irrational base, the accumulation of faults, errors, and psychological deficiencies that not only kept him in the utmost and complete disorientation, but also constituted the cause of his moral and spiritual failings.

One can see now how Logosophy penetrates deeply into the meaning of each word, expression or concept that man has heard and still hears without having its content clearly explained to him.

We have said that the spiritual entity dies being consumed by inertia, a fact that having been sensed in past eras, has given way to the belief that during this phase the spirit suffers the torments of its annihilation. We will not comment on this point now, because it pertains to a different category of statements. The truth is that the imagination of those who felt such intuition were led to portray the supposed torment as the "flames of hell"; since then, it has been repeated that "the spirits who sin burn eternally" in the infernal fires. Logosophy declares and sustains that since the spirits are immaterial they are also incombustible and in the event such a tremendous and reckless affirmation is accepted, one can only confirm, that having eternally resisted the effect of the flames, the spirit has proven its absolute immunity to combustion. On the other hand, how could the human soul conceive of justice in God if such sacrifice were permitted? And what would be His objective?

Nevertheless, one must ask: Is it possible that God, who created the infinite immensity of the worlds, who has inserted in the atom a marvelous mechanism, could allow the souls created by Him to burn eternally? This, therefore, is an unusual and inadmissibly vindictive pronouncement which depicts such a merciless God; a God who can exist only in the hallucinated minds of those who invented this enormous fabrication.

We have alluded to one of the many depressing images used to terrorize one's soul and, in so doing, influences it and deeply harms one's faculty of reasoning. In pointing out this error, our word frees with irrefutable logic the individual conscience from such a blindly accepted absurdity.

One of the causes, perhaps the main one responsible for the annihilation of the spirit, that is the second death, is the atrophy of the faculties of the intelligence, especially the faculties of thinking, of reasoning and of observing. And it is so, because by not functioning as they should, they gradually annul the human ability to survive since they close the doors to the occurrence of the spirit. The fanatical or blind beliefs have contributed to a maximum degree towards this end. Man, accustomed since childhood to seek guardianship for his soul, becomes spiritually incapacitated to be self-sufficient. Today he struggles between the slavery of mental molds that depress him and the yearnings for knowledge, with no other alternative than to limit his thinking to what he barely needed to move in the material world. He is not capable of giving the spiritual being the preponderant place it must occupy in his life and consequently its evolution throughout the centuries is postponed and detained.

Logosophical science has the proven virtue of awakening the faculties of the intelligence; and not only does it awaken them, but moves them into action. When these faculties break through the barriers of internal submission, man conquers the much longed for freedom of conscience, while his faculty of reasoning is mobilized and he acquires confidence in the elaboration of his judgments, a confidence that protects him against any deceit, against any mystification, wherever it may come from.

In cases of acute numbness, the spirit remains absent, prevented from exercising any constructive activity because the mental system functions so defectively, that it becomes impossible for it to participate in any way in the person's life. A similar thing occurs in those people who have surrendered their individuality by allowing themselves to be absorbed by the masses. Converted into mass-men, they lose all possibility of receiving even the smallest assistance from their own spirit. This spiritual assistance is effectively interrupted since the mind of the mass-man does not obey his own will, but rather the will of others. He only obeys those who impose upon him their dictates with the threat of severe reprisals.

People who live under these conditions are rarely able to recover their individuality by themselves.

Their lives have retrogressed to eras that must be overcome if they wish to avoid being left behind in the evolutionary journey. Nevertheless, we are hopeful that the logosophical cognitions as stimulating, as they are fecund, will finally be able to awaken within them, the yearning to be free and to be masters of their own destinies, since man's right to grow freely cannot be denied, so that the traits of his spirit are allowed to flow within him in plenitude.

We have established in this chapter that the human spirit, whose life lasts throughout each period of physical existence, can nevertheless succumb and reach total disintegration. A sad end for he who ignores or does not take into account that a better destiny had been reserved for him. Faced with this demoralizing scenario displayed by these people, it is undoubtedly rewarding and awakens our optimism to know that when life is sustained and strengthened by cognitions that nourish its perpetuity, the spirit continues its existence, because it would have been given the necessary forces to live forever. Therefore, one cannot deny what we have been saying repeatedly, and that is: The person who carries out the true function of life, overcoming all the contingencies that could emerge during his journey on earth, forges a destiny superior to that commonly achieved by others; an ample destiny, flooded by the light of truths which are conquered and elevated to the highest level by the immanent presence of the spirit.

Chapter 18

MISDIRECTIONS

It is logical to think that the truths descend from above as human beings come to need or deserve them. At a certain level of the descent, the truths separate and, while a part breaks away and manifests itself in the material world, the rest remain on the mental, spiritual or metaphysical plane. This generates the two realities that form the truth, one physical and the other spiritual; the latter is prominent and is the one that lasts through the ages, because it is consubstantiated with the very core of Creation. As they both stem from the same essence it is noteworthy to observe that one is as real as the other, inasmuch as the physical truth is released from the spiritual. Now then, the conformation of the human mind does not permit the human being to penetrate the spiritual plane without having previously reached the necessary degree of self-betterment to avoid getting lost. We are aware of the short or long term sanctions that apply when a reckless action is used to penetrate it, that is, the loss of reasoning and the disconnection of the human sensitivity from the physical and spiritual reality. One should never forget that everything in creation is natural and, when someone tries to force it by building one concept or another that is removed from reality, the sanctions emerge.

Our objective is to teach the truth. Hence, we consider it necessary to clarify what has constituted an obsession to many unprepared souls and even to some scientists. We are referring to the so-called "spiritualistic practices" which received a favorable response from people during the last century as a result its novelty. A limited number of scientists believed they had found the path that would lead them to remarkable discoveries and delved into the investigation of the phenomenalistic actions of the mediums. However, we do not discard the idea that they were moved by a desire to snatch away some secret from the sphinx of the metaphysical

* N.T.: The author is referring to the 19th Century.

154

world, but nothing of the sort happened. On the contrary, several of them surrendered to the temptation of feeling the effects, not at all positive, of the power of suggestion produced by the gloomy environment, as well as the murmurs and the contortions exhibited by the "possessed".

Many years have passed since such expectations first began, without any serious confirmation having been obtained to date, any progress that would at least point to something of the truth as a result of the investigations. Sectarian groups or pseudo-spiritualistic societies still insist on demonstrating, through questionable means, metaphysical occurrences that are nothing more than mere imaginative and chimerical visions.

Let us now explain, since we deem it indispensable for a broader comprehension of what we previously explained about the spirit, that it is not possible to gloss over the enormous absurdities raised about the subject. In effect, it has been said and continues to be claimed insistently amongst spiritualistic groups, that the people who join these groups seeking consolation communicate with the spirits of dead people by means of a medium. In order to destroy such an outright invention, it would suffice to remember that the laws which govern man's psychic and mental life prohibit transgressions of any kind. The notion of calling the spirits of others to make use of our physical entity is so absurd, that we are compelled to ask people to reflect and to use common sense. One should note that if the medium remains extraneous to the knowledge of his own spirit – as demonstrated by his total ignorance – if he has never tried to conduct a serious and sensible investigation of his spirit, he cannot attribute to himself the privilege of access to "the beyond", nor expect that the spirits of others come to him, possess his physical being and be used to display a ridiculous spectacle devoid of any credibility. Could it be that the people who practice spiritualism have no notion at all of the respect due to the pain felt by relatives and to the memory of the deceased?

As the successors of the ancient necromancy, today's spiritualists base their beliefs upon the uncontrolled manifestations of their mediums, which according to their followers, once the possessed is in "trance", he invokes the spirit that has been requested to come to him, makes it manifest itself in him and express his desires and thoughts. It behooves me to ask at this point if it's possible for a person who is barely educated, who is totally ignorant of the universal laws, who has not been able to experience within himself the presence of his spirit, to subject to his whim the spirits of others or even worse, as sometimes claimed, of those superior to his? Or could it be that one seeks to deceive in some way our sense of reasoning in order to conform to certain thoughts that obsess us? The same thing happened to the Hebrew, Saul, when, according to the Scriptures, he invoked Samuel's shadow using the pythoness of Endor.

It is surely the imagination that plays the leading role in this kind of chimerical vision. It is well known that superstition comes from way back. It emerged in the obscurantism that governed remote times, influencing even the most outstanding personalities of the time. Ulysses' evocation at Tiresias, as narrated by Homer, demonstrates the exaltation of the hero who seeks, more than the apparition of the specter, the inspiration of the fortune teller. Although this is mere fiction, it is interesting to note the subtlety of the wise Greek poet who preferred the possible to the impossible.

If everything we have said up to now has still not clarified the issue, we would add that assuming the experiences of the mediums were real, if it were so easy for them to establish contact with the beyond, how many things of incalculable transcendence in the metaphysical world would already be known to mankind? And yet the fact that we still remain in the dark about this issue is proof of the audacity of such a childish mystification. This should truly convince everyone that no matter how attractive it may be, no phenomenic spectacle could ever conform to one's judgment, nor to one's conscience, and to a far lesser degree to anyone's spirit.

Chapter 19

ON ETERNAL REST

Throughout this task, and maintaining our unvarying working method, we have not departed an iota from its straightforward and convincing design, as is demanded by the transcendence of the subjects addressed in each chapter, the vital importance of which to man's future and that of mankind, can be instantly perceived. Our word, permanently supported by the force that generates the truths upon which Logosophy is based, has a life-giving and constructive power that directly and efficiently influences the human soul.

Let us now refer to a certain predicament which has been deeply rooted for thousands of years: that is the "eternal rest" which is wished to any spirit when leaving this world. But first, we would like to pose three questions in the name of common sense and logic:

1) Is there anyone who, during a period of physical life – ephemeral tin relation to the infinity of cosmic time – would have worked so hard as to deserve such idleness?

2) How can an evolved spirit consent to withdraw itself into everlasting uselessness, while so many human souls, whom it could help, suffer in the world?

3) Who could aspire to eternal rest knowing that his spirit must continue the evolution pre-established by law?

As far as we are concerned, we would be very grateful if we were wished eternal activity, since activity is energy and energy is the engine that drives our existence in any of its manifestations. Eternal rest, on the other hand, is immobility, the second death, chaos, nothingness. While activity broadens life, inertia compresses it with the risk of losing it.

From the above one can deduce that unknowingly one would express a negative thought towards a person to whom "eternal rest" is wished. We consider this, therefore, as clear proof of how extraneous certain communities are regarding the reality that Logosophy unveils about conscious evolution, which presents a cognition that provides a basic notion of the possible perpetuity of the spirit throughout all the cycles of its existence.

Every human being who deems himself to be one, in the highest expression of its meaning, must sense that his creation obeys a superior purpose and therefore cannot limit his life to the routine-like and simple tasks of living and dying under the influence of a materialistic conception, which concedes nothing more than the common prerogatives of a mere daily existence. Man's fundamental activity, the one he performs above and beyond his physical or material duties, must be dedicated to obtaining highly constructive experiences for his evolution. How? By taking a strong interest in leading his conscious life towards a destiny that completely transcends the common one. Our science fulfills this aspiration entirely and guides each individual to penetrate deeply into the mysteries of his own existence.

Having thus swept away all doubt, one acquires the certainty that neither during life, nor in the afterlife, would a prolonged rest be convenient for anyone. Inertia disintegrates matter and that same law applies to the individual spirit.

God cannot encourage life in those souls who contradict the great law of evolution which fills the universe with energy and which is permanent activity. One must enjoy the activity, in this case, conscious activity, since we are referring to the one preferred by the spirit. This is the activity that makes us experience the constant flow of life, because it promotes the link with the energy of creation, which is the imperceptible yet fecund breath that gives stability to everything that exists.

When the spirit is sustained by the ever-active elements of eternity it becomes invulnerable to the passing of time, which never affects that which remains active, lively, and united to the breath of universal life.

We trust that the reader has been able to appreciate the importance of our cognitions, which allow one to experience the sensation of eternity from within this physical plane, just by knowing that time measured in hours can be expanded, while life is lived intensively, deeply, and fully.

PART TWO

Five preliminary questions

Are dreams the faithful reflection of a reality that is still out of our reach?

What values has man obtained from his attempted interpretations of dreams without knowing their true dimensions and ranges?

What occurs on the fringes of our senses and our conscience in the penumbra of our daily circumstances?

While asleep what manages our mental faculties which produce and reproduce events that make us experience sensations as real as those that occur during our vigil, or frequently jars our sensitivity?

How can we consciously register these metaphysical occurrences or events, when our senses cease their task and we lose all connection with the reality that surrounds us?

Access to the truth can only be obtained through cognitions that dispel the shadows of uncertainty. The dreams cannot escape this law; consequently, it is through this same conduit that man will have to discover the grand agent that promotes them.

Chapter 20

THE SPIRIT AS THE DETERMINING FACTOR OF DREAMS

Everybody is aware of how much has been said and written about dreams. Numerous works and authors have attempted to explain and interpret them, and around this enigmatic psychic expression – phenomenal to some – all sorts of conjectures have been made. The truth is that nobody to date has clarified the mystery that dreams present to the human intelligence, and the efforts made until now have been lost in the obscurity that surrounds its physiognomy.

Our objective is to dedicate part of this book to such an unsettled question in order to explain the dimension given to it by the logosophical conception, and its logical and transcendental significance as a fact that must vividly interest the human conscience.

For the sake of clarifying further the disclosures that follow, we will start from a point that is perfectly established: that one thing is the act of sleeping and another, very different, is the function of dreaming. Frequently, people are accustomed to saying "during my dreams", meaning "while I was asleep", which results in a univocal reference of two sentences of different context. It is known that sleeping is a somatic necessity imposed by the law of conservation that regulates the biological function of the human organism. Dreaming, on the other hand, responds to other needs, not precisely physical, but of the spirit.

We assert that the faculty of dreaming is exclusive to the spirit because it alone uses it and, of course, knows how to use it. It is, par excellence, the instrument used by the spirit to satisfy the important needs of its governing function. This function starts to be perceived by man by virtue of the process of conscious evolution which promotes, as was clearly expressed in previous chapters, the gradual contact between the physical being and the spirit. To perform such a function the spirit uses the faculties of the intelligence of the inferior or common mind[1] as well as the thoughts contained in it, in order not only to get to know the actions of the physical being and extract from them all that is positive, but also to activate or guide the faculties of the superior mind to observe the thoughts that rallied in it.

Man knows that he dreams but ignores that dreaming is a faculty of the mind; a faculty which, at the same time, constitutes one of the greatest prerogatives given to human intelligence. Therefore, we are not dealing here with a faculty similar to those that integrate the intelligence in accordance with what we specified in other books when we referred to the mental system. And it is not similar, because it acts without the intervention of the senses and outside the individual's will; it even disregards the conscience itself when it lacks the cognitions that allow it to embrace the spirit's activities. Instead, it uses the faculties of the intelligence, and of the sensitive and instinctive systems. More than a faculty, dreaming is the power that assists the spirit in using the mind and its other psychological resources offered by the physical entity while it sleeps and guides him in his evolution.

[1] See "Logosophy, Science and Method" (Lesson III) by the same author.

Dreams are, therefore, the results of the individual spirit's intervention which produces them while the person is asleep. When one becomes conscious of one's dreams, they will be the evidence of what man can achieve during his vigil, as long as he seeks to establish the link between his spirit and his conscience.

Just the fact of knowing the existence of the faculty of dreaming, of knowing at least something related to its wonderful functions, will help us to think seriously about this prodigious creation, which is man himself, endowed with a psychological mechanism that when organized, will make him feel the happiest of all beings.

Innumerable conjectures have been made about dreams. Many have tried to decipher them, to assign to them a specific meaning; still many more have woven around them fantastic conjectures, but nobody has ever stated that they are produced by the spirit in its constant effort to be present in our daily existence.

We have, therefore, established that the spirit notwithstanding its inevitable exclusion from man's vigil, due to the latter's ignorance of its mission, lends its assistance to man while he sleeps by way of the faculty of dreaming. We repeat: When the physical being is asleep, it is the spirit which manages his mental mechanism. One should take this into account in order to better understand the reality that we are presenting.

The aforesaid statements confirm that since our senses do not participate in any way during sleep and our conscious and rational activities are suspended, something uses our mind and makes us feel upon awakening, the exact sensation of having lived, without the assistance of our will, through a psychic and mental experience, so lucid at times, that its events can be remembered during our vigil as if we had in reality lived them. This something, we insist, can be nothing other than one's own spirit, which promotes the experiences in the metaphysical sphere. It is easy to observe that some faculties of the intelligence act with the same dynamic force that activate them during our vigil, but they do so directed by the spirit; for example, the faculty of remembering, which is required in this type of extra conscious experience as the means for the individual to register what happened, or what he did in his dreams, whether it be for good or evil.

This does not constitute a mystery to anybody, as proven by the sensations that remain from our dreams when we wake up. However, it does reveal a fact of paramount transcendence in our lives. If the spirit seeks to communicate with our conscience and uses the resources offered by our psychic nature on the fringe of our will, should we not respond to the invitation it repeatedly sends to our feeling and thinking by turning towards it, so that it can reign over our inner selves now, after having maintained it in the most deplorable exile? We said "exile" because in fact, due to human ignorance, the spirit suffered a deplorable displacement or banishment. Nevertheless, as any exile yearns to return to his familiar environment so does the spirit seek to be present in some way in our life and it does so without infringing the laws, that is, in a way that is most adequate to its incorporeal nature.

Dreams can be lucid or confused. When the faculty of dreaming connects with the consciousness, even circumstantially, the dreams are lucid; if it does not, then the dreams are confused, because memory, extraneous in these cases to the functions of the faculty of dreaming, cannot clearly retain what was dreamt after one wakes up. It is the imagination, therefore, that supplements the dream with twisted elements thus distorting the retained image and altering even further its physiognomy. On other occasions, upon awakening, one has the sensation of having suffered a horrible and disturbing nightmare[2] without being able to explain the causes that provoked it.

It is rare to maintain a lucid memory of a happy dream. Bearing this in mind, one will better understand the importance of organizing the mental system and of exercising supervision over the thoughts used during our daily chores and activities, in order to avoid that our dreams be reduced to vague and often insipid recollections.

We frequently awaken with the impression of having dreamed nonsense, without thinking that what passes through one's mind during the day has more or less the same characteristics. To confirm this, one could jot down what goes on in one's mind from the moment one wakes up to bedtime, and will notice the enormous range of events that frequently wander back and forth, as for example, curiosity expressed with interest, with concern, with prejudice,

[2] In our book, "The Mechanism of Conscious Life", we have addressed at length the characteristics of certain dreams and their logosophical explanation, as well as the cases of somnambulism, nightmares, etc.

with doubts, etc., including those instances when the mental retina is etched, amongst other things, by thoughts instigated by the instinct, agitated by the exaltation of passions, or the frenzy of heated arguments. During the day, in short, most people, with few exceptions, neither follow an orderly sequence in their mental activity nor consciously coordinate their actions. We see how serious matters are intermingled with jokes, with memories of this or that dubious event, with malicious anecdotes and all that which one listens to during one's daily contacts, which often contaminate the mind, without mentioning all the thoughts that often involve one's behavior. Hence by projecting on a panoramic screen all that which runs through the mind during one day, we would have the exact duplication of our wildest dreams. This proves to what extent the physical being takes into account its inner reality demonstrating quite obviously that his conscience would neither act in a timely fashion nor with the necessary speed during each moment of his life if it were not trained towards the fulfillment of such a lofty role. This demonstration confirms our thesis that assigns to the inheritance collected by the spirit, after each earthly experiment, a value in line with the use that one has made of his life. Therefore, having noticed the meager evolutionary result we have been able to gather, it is not difficult to deduce how disappointing it must be for the imponderable custodian of our individual asset to absorb such meager results. But we could also gauge the extraordinary changes that would occur in favor of the human creature, if today's man were to apply the same energy and efforts he devotes to his material progress, towards increasing the potential resources of his spirit.

During these extra conscious experiences called "dreams", strange episodes occur outside all voluntary participation of our senses. Some are accustomed to see themselves accomplishing deeds that startle them, sometimes in shame and other times in horror, due to the sensations that last even after waking up. These dreams are seemingly unexplainable and are rejected by our sensitivity, as we feel repulsed by such manifestations. The fact is that we are unaware that these were produced by some remote reminiscence. On the other hand, it is easy to recognize oneself in the dreams that reproduce the thoughts that were predominant during one's vigil, such as those that promoted some morbid, criminal, infamous, or just erroneous intentions. The spirit, which knows them to be dangerous, takes them and, by magnifying their effect, projects in the being it animates the image of what would happen if the individual allowed himself to be seduced by them. And even though the faculty of remembering is not able to maintain the vision of what was dreamt, the individual's sensitivity is often moved and strengthened by virtue of this repelling of all attempts to subvert the feeling or divert the willpower.

A vehement desire left unsatisfied, a certain ambition cut short, or a frustrated excitement of the inner centers often leave psychic consequences in the individual. In addition to the above, we often have our instinctive system participate, disturbing the movements of the intelligence. This is commonly called "blockage". The individual suppresses movement that would liberate him from the need he experiences, or from the thought that disturbs him. Observing him, the spirit intervenes to protect him against the damage that his undefined inner conflict could cause him and this is when, by virtue of its mediation, the psychic relief occurs in the individual, reproducing in the dream those images that constitute the course of said conflict.

The spirit usually participates in such cases, using at the same time two forms equally constructive. While on one hand it delights the physical being by making him achieve what he suppressed during his vigil, on the other hand, it warns him of the inconvenience of fomenting or cajoling his senses with certain thoughts. Thus, liberated during his dream by his own spirit, the individual conserves upon waking up the sensation of a new understanding that helps him define other forms of conduct; and even in the cases in which he does not clearly perceive it, he finds it strange that he dared allow such desires to occur.

These dreams of misconduct or lewdness are explainable if one takes into account that the spirit, which animates the physical being, not only knows what the latter thinks or does, but also knows the systems that constitute his psychology, which it uses as a conduit to extend its assistance to him.

Not all that happens in man's mental scenario while he sleeps is of the sort described above, but the fact is that all cases carry an educational objective which tends to favor the evolutionary development of the individual even when he ignores it or lacks the capability or resources to interpret it. When one lives completely divorced from one's spirit it is undoubtedly difficult to understand the importance of the dreams, since these require the assistance of cognitions that would eliminate any possibility of their absurd interpretations.

The images that appear in the dreams vibrate in time; the sort of time that is not measured in hours. The events reproduced in the dreams may not have necessarily occurred yesterday or today; they could reflect events that happened ten years ago or even in more remote eras. These images sometimes linger throughout epochs in the translucence of the conscience, projecting an event that was lived, a moment of pleasure, an imagined delight, a fear, a painful episode, etc. These images are reproduced at an opportune time by the spirit in the individual by means of the faculty of dreaming; and it does so in order for the individual to achieve a clear notion of a reality or a truth that he needs to know, which otherwise would be difficult to obtain without such a recourse.

There are dreams in which the images take on symbolic forms and their interpretation require a laborious and deep investigation. In these cases, the importance of the transcendent cognitions become evident as they offer the keys to the analogies which not only help to decipher them, but also favor the use of their content as a message to orient one's life. Noteworthy here is the paramount participation of sensitivity as the inductive force capable of directing the faculties of the intelligence to interpret what was dreamt. Let us now examine the following case: A person who wants to successfully overcome threatening difficulties finds himself in his dreams navigating in a stormy sea. The frail boat in which he sails, whipped by the storm, ends by sinking. In this critical situation he remembers that he does not know how to swim, yet, at the same time, he notices that he is not afraid; his body floats and easily resists the onslaught of the sea. He suddenly realizes that he is in extreme danger as he feels himself being strongly pulled down to the deep by someone else who, on the point of drowning, clings to his clothes. At first he considers himself lost, but just in time remembers that he possesses resources to face this emergency, and after extreme effort finds himself once again floating on the surface and finally stepping on firm land. Upon waking up, he feels a sensation of joy and of profound relief.

It would not be difficult to perceive the link between this symbolic dream and the concerns of our protagonist. Following this first step and taking into account the sensible advice previously mentioned, the exact interpretation of the message in the dream and its future application will occur. Said application consists in preparing oneself against possible adverse events and to be able to use the recourse offered to overcome them, which one will find in the timely use of the means given by one's own spirit to survive any difficulty or catastrophe no matter how serious it may be.

We will now address dreams of magnificent effects in which the physical being experiences the delights of being transported to uncommon scenarios. One generally sees oneself moving as if scaling towering heights or savoring long-awaited conquests; in these cases the spirit usually exalts the thoughts that define the aspirations of the physical being. During the subtle path covered by these visions, the spirit expressly enhances the beauty of the images therein contained, so that the physical being is able later on to conserve the most inexpressible sensations of what was dreamed. Its objective, easy to understand, is none other than to transfer to life all that the physical being was able to retain from his dreams, parts of which will constitute the basis and the stimulus for his efforts in achieving the noble objective that vibrates in them.

Many believe that such objectives are unattainable and considered to be beyond their possibilities – something similar to the veil of Queen Mab – without thinking that everything is possible to man when he understands the world of the cognitions that must be the specific bases of each one of his achievements.

The belief of the unattainable can be clearly seen in certain exclamations of pleasure, admiration, or of intense outbursts of happiness or joy, as for instance: "It's like a dream come true!"; "I thought I was dreaming"; "This can only happen in dreams" which expressly define how much all this seems to be beyond human prerogatives. The individual himself is the first to feel extraneous to what he is experiencing, which implicitly makes him realize that the happiness he experienced in his dreams exceeds that which is generated by the joyful events of his daily life. This means that certain events are considered by man to be out of the ordinary and of such eloquence that they exceed the limits of his imagination, yet experiencing the sensation that these extraordinary moments of his life go beyond his immediate perceptions. There is no doubt that between the sublime ecstasy produced by the dreams and that which the reality of daily life produces, there is a notable difference. In the dreams it is the spirit which makes the sensitivity experience the beauty. In the reality of daily life, except in those cases where the spirit participates in the life of the individual, this fact is solely due to the exaltation of the senses.

We have been able to observe frequently that the spirit activates the faculty of dreaming in very special moments during our vigil; moments that have been called "daydreams", in which for a fleeting moment, thoughts soar to lofty heights and delight us in the contemplation of exquisite abstractions. The father who lets his thought of good health fly on the wings of a daydream nursed by the yearning of seeing his sick son recover; or the individual who delves into the contemplation of infinity, anxious to discover what lies beyond the terrestrial ties. Does not one and the other lose sight of all the physical connections that surround them to plunge into what constitutes the depth of their thoughts? In this state of abstraction, do they not both escape all physical sensation to live this brief moment of ecstasy, one attached by remote hopes and the other by secret reminiscences? Their physical eyes see nothing. Many things can parade in front of them and yet nothing can interrupt the images that absorb them because their sight, in these cases, looks in another direction, remaining very closely linked to thought. Therefore, we have a fact here that was produced as a result of a strong yearning, of a profound desire of the individual. And the spirit responded by means of the daydream through which the mind could enrich itself with the appropriate elements for the individual's future and destiny.

The foregoing implies that although man does not manifest a true concern towards knowing his spirit and to seal his unity with it, the spirit uses every appropriate opportunity to encourage him, to protect and assist him in his many difficult moments and prove to him during meaningful circumstances that it is the spirit, and uniquely the spirit, which manifests itself and intervenes indirectly as in the above instances. Far from being a chimerical creation, the spirit, being as real as the physical being, logically feels and experiences the same as the latter – the sensations and other facts that occur in man's life. The spirit is not amazed by what man does or does not do in the material or physical plane where he acts, but always, as long as man lives, it protects him and extends its assistance in multiple ways, so that man does not abuse his prerogatives and conserves, if not the memory, at least a sensation of his extraterrestrial origin.

Chapter 21

HOW CAN MAN BECOME A CONSCIOUS SPECTATOR OF HIS DREAMS?

Logosophy answers this question with a categorical affirmation, but with the condition that man must undertake the process of conscious evolution, because conscience cannot act in the dreams without having been previously trained and equipped with essential cognitions that enable it to fulfill this function. In honesty and common sense one cannot conceive that the human being would seek, out of mere curiosity or through sheer speculation, the knowledge of a secret uniquely reserved for those who, having acquired it, would never use it for petty ends which are always tainted with personal vanity. The cognitions acquired by means of conscious evolution carry a responsibility that is impossible to avoid since it would be prevented by the incorruptible character of the conscience.

Nevertheless, we will now explain the mechanism which makes it possible, with due caution, to pass through the doors which provide access to this hermetic secret, one of so many that man has not yet been able to uncover.

We will start by calling attention to a fact that occurs with relative frequency in the life of many people and from which no conclusion has been drawn. We refer to the state of being "half asleep" that has been often trivially overlooked as being totally unimportant. In the state of being "half asleep" in which one experiences drowsiness just before the act of sleeping, our senses continue to act. During those moments, however, the action of the senses is not continuous as during the vigil, but fluctuates between fleeting moments of sensorial perception and moments of delving into the mental penumbra. One has the feeling of being asleep, although not totally, since one is aware of one's surroundings; the eyes open and are able to see if one wanted to.

Very well. This state of "half asleep" has a short duration, although in some cases it is usually extended by the resistance put up by some serious concern that opposes the physiological need of our

body to rest. Because of this, the faculties of thinking or imagining usually maintain their activities
struggling to overcome sleep; or else it would be the
thoughts as mental agents that prolong the vigil in
view of settling some difficult problem that had not
been resolved. All this produces a cerebral and
nervous excitement which, in a way, propitiates the
necessary relaxation towards the act of sleeping
which occurs when the mental activity ceases, as the
energetic power that sustained it has been exhausted.
Finally one goes to sleep, becoming totally removed
from the surrounding world.

The importance here is to indicate that the state
of "half asleep" occurs during those fleeting moments
in which the activity of the mental faculties or that
of the thoughts seem to interfere with the attempt
to sleep, giving rise to moments of thinking and
moments of sleeping inducing one to confuse the
images generated by one plane or another.

When man undertakes the process of conscious
evolution as proposed by Logosophy and already
reaches a certain level of advanced conscience, he
will be able to successfully attempt to exercise a
conscious self-control over those moments in which

sleep interferes with the mental activity that makes the senses tense. The state of "half asleep", in this case, can become the conduit through which one can consciously manage the alternatives of the dream.

To observe and monitor with plenitude of conscience what occurs during the state of "half asleep", having sufficient control to extract one's self from the action of the senses, that is, with total abstraction from the external sensations, allows one to explore from this position the regions of sleep and within them focus on the impetus of the will.

Such attempts are conducive to a gradual knowledge of how the mind works during dreams, when the spirit uses the faculty of dreaming. The person who has achieved this knows that when he rests his head on the pillow, he deposits on it a treasure. He knows that before sleeping he must calm his mind so that the faculty of dreaming can act unhindered. He also knows how to create in himself the most elevated state of mind so that nothing disturbs the work to be done by this faculty to which he seeks to get closer. In short, he would have succeeded in gathering several useful resources that not only would allow him to assist the faculty of dreaming, but also to trust its power of achievement in that he expects it to answer the intimate call that undoubtedly will enlighten with greater vigor his intelligence.

It is of paramount importance that the systems that make up human psychology function well, in order that the vision of the activity deployed under the influence of the faculty of dreaming is clearly retained. It now becomes easier to recognize that if a greater agility of the faculties of our mind increases the efficiency of our actions during our vigil, that same agility will also enhance the performance of said faculties during our sleep.

We have already stated that the sensitivity is responsible for a good part of the blurred recollection of what was dreamt and for the sensations that the individual retains when he awakes. It is, therefore, logical to expect that these sensations become far clearer and precise once the sensitive system is conveniently organized, and even more so if we perceive that associated with the improved functions of the sensitive system is the mental system with its faculties, now in an advanced stage of development, all of which results in a greater efficiency of both systems during our sleep. This infers, therefore, that through the process of conscious evolution dreams become clearer, more peaceful and more real.

When the faculties of the intelligence perform their true conscious function during the vigil or, in other words, when the three systems that constitute the psychological being interrelate harmoniously, then the spirit will reign over the life of the individual. The faculty of dreaming, which until then operated only when the individual was asleep, could now prolong its action even during the vigil by projecting the images experienced during the dream. This means that the individual has access to the faculty of dreaming, which will respond obediently to the orders of the intelligence. This faculty, which we will also call the "key faculty", has now been able to synchronize both mental movements, that of dreaming and that of being awake. Thus, an understanding, a relationship has been produced between the physical being and the spirit, which now liberated, uses the faculties of the mind and the other systems during the vigil, allowing in turn the physical being to remember everything that happened while he was under the influence of the faculty of dreaming.

We would like now to repeat what we said at the beginning of this chapter: Everything that man investigates concerning his spirit, trying to discover what its activity consists of and its form of manifestation, must not constitute isolated facts or be motivated by curiosity which leads nowhere, but rather must represent the sum of a series of observations and proven facts, such as those brought forth by the process of conscious evolution. This subjective formality, when applied to each phase of this process, will accentuate the possibilities of penetrating it with one's own understanding. This is the only way by which one could incorporate to one's conscious inheritance the irreversible result of the acquired knowledge, since it is precisely this same knowledge which forges the granitic bases of our destiny.

To be able to consciously manage the faculty of dreaming implies having reached one of the greatest evolutionary triumphs reserved to man: the integration of the psychophysical being with his spirit.

With this we also answer the question posed by Aristotle some two thousand four hundred years ago, when he asked himself how the spirit could be united to the body.

FINAL WORDS

The great thruts have their most sublime expression in the precise dimension of their cosmic projections, in the infinite wisdom of their universal content and in their ineffable simplicity.

The logosophical conception bases its precepts upon this transcendent and inalterable order, and it is for this reason that the cognitions it radiates open deep furrows in the human soul, uprooting the evil grass of superstition and credulity, so that the cereal of life may sprout with vigor, and flourish, free from all evil contamination.

No human being in whom the spirit has ceased to be a myth, but instead has become a potent force of his own existence's designs, could ignore the immense good that such designs will provide him. He will no longer be a man with remnants of the savage, ignorant of himself, a pariah of truth and good, because he would have consummated through his evolutionary exploit the lofty content of the conscious emancipation of his spirit.

When the spirit reigns within each man, when it ceases to be an abstract being to convert into a living presence of his human existence, then everything will fundamentally change for his own good within the bosom of his species. Only then will man be able to grasp and achieve his grand mission, fully conscious of his responsibility before God and before himself.

The reign of the spirit amongst men will then be the reign of understanding, of tolerance, of order, and of truth itself. This, however, will not happen overnight from one day to the next. Before that, man will have to fight tirelessly with full conviction of his final triumph. The man who has been deceived, who has suffered the iniquities of an unjustifiable mental and moral slavery, will shake off the yoke of his immense misfortune and will join the armies that will march victorious through all the paths of the world, proclaiming this truth that will make all human beings free and conscious of their great human mission, which is spiritual and eternal.

Table of Contents

❦

PART ONE

The Spirit

❦

PART TWO

The Dreams

Regional Representatives

Belo Horizonte
Rua Piauí, 742 – Funcionários
30150-320 – Belo Horizonte – MG
Fone (31) 3273 1717

Brasília
SHCG/NORTE – Quadra 704 – Área de Escolas
70730-730 – Brasília – DF
Fone (61) 3326 4205

Chapecó
Rua Clevelândia, 1389 D – Saic
89802-411 – Chapecó – SC
Fone (49) 3322 5514

Curitiba
Rua Almirante Gonçalves, 2081 – Rebouças
80250-150 – Curitiba – PR
Fone (41) 3332 2814

Florianópolis
Rua Deputado Antonio Edu Vieira, 150 – B. Pantanal
88040-000 – Florianópolis – SC
Fone (48) 3333 6897

Goiânia
Av. São João, 311 – Q 13 Lote 23 E – B. Alto da Glória
74815-280 – Goiânia – GO
Fone (62) 3281 9413

Rio de Janeiro
Rua General Polidoro, 36 – B. Botafogo
22280-001 – Rio de Janeiro – RJ
Fone (21) 2543 1138

São Paulo
Rua Gal. Chagas Santos, 590 – Saúde
04146-051 – São Paulo – SP
Fone (11) 5584 6648

Uberlândia
Rua Alexandre de Oliveira Marquez, 113 – B. Vigilato Pereira
38400-256 – Uberlândia – MG
Fone (34) 3237 1130